410592

327.73   Fincher, Ernest
FIN   Barksdale.

Mexico and the
United States, their
linked destinies.

YELM HIGH SCHOOL LIBRARY
YELM WA 98597

MEXICO
and the
UNITED
STATES

MEXICO
and the
UNITED STATES

Their Linked Destinies

E. B. FINCHER

illustrated with photographs

THOMAS Y. CROWELL NEW YORK

For Almyra and Hugh

For information address Thomas Y. Crowell Junior Books,
10 East 53 Street, New York, N. Y. 10022.
Published simultaneously in Canada by
Fitzhenry & Whiteside Limited, Toronto.
1 2 3 4 5 6 7 8 9 10
First Edition

Library of Congress Cataloging in Publication Data
Fincher, Ernest Barksdale, 1910–
   Mexico and the United States, their linked
destinies.

   Bibliography: p.
   Includes index.
   Summary: A study of the historical relationship
between the United States and Mexico, with particular
emphasis on Mexico's emerging role as a world leader.
   1. United States—Foreign relations—Mexico—Juvenile
literature. 2. Mexico—Foreign relations—United States—
Juvenile literature. [1. United States—Foreign relations
—Mexico. 2. Mexico—Foreign relations—United States]
I. Title.
E183.8.M6F54 1983   327.73072   82–45581
ISBN 0-690-04310-4
ISBN 0-690-04311-2 (lib. bdg.)

Contents

ACKNOWLEDGMENTS

The theme of this book was first suggested by Manuel Sán-chez Gavito. One of his lectures at the National Preparatory School in Mexico City dealt with "The American Inva-sion"—his term for what I had been taught was the Mexican War. For a moment, the title of the lecture gave offense, but it soon became apparent that the war between the speak-er's country and my own was to be discussed with clinical objectivity. Later, with Sánchez Gavito as my guide, I com-pared chapters dealing with the war of 1846–1848 in Mexi-can textbooks with the treatment of that conflict in textbooks published in the United States. Seemingly, the Mexican and American writers were not describing the same war. At the time, I wondered whether it was possible to write a book on Mexican-American relations that would be accepted as a fair statement on both sides of the Rio Grande. *Mexico and the United States: Their Linked Destinies* represents my effort to write such a book.

My thinking has been influenced by the comments on Mexican-American relations made by Alejandro Barbajosa during a seminar at the National Autonomous University in Mexico City some years ago. Having spent considerable time in the United States, this Spanish-born Mexican had special insights to share with Americans. More recently, another young Mexican, Rafael Palafox, a leader of the Institutional Revolutionary Party (PRI) in the state of Guanajuato, has helped clarify my thinking on Mexican-American relations.

In acknowledging debts, the author of a book of this kind thinks of the many librarians who have given generously of their time and expertise. The staffs of The Library of Congress, El Colegio de Mexico, the Organization of American States, the Brookings Institution, and the New York Public Library have been especially helpful to me. I also am indebted to Charles Alvarez of the Inter-American Development Bank, who assisted in the collection of illustrations for this book.

I have been fortunate in having my colleague, Robert R. Parsons, as my critic at every stage in the writing of this book. It goes without saying, however, that for any errors of fact or interpretation the responsibility is entirely mine.

—E. B. Fincher

MEXICO and the UNITED STATES

Views Across the Border

"Poor Mexico, so far from God, so close to the United States" is a wry expression that Mexicans sometimes use to describe the relationship between their country and its powerful neighbor.

The preoccupation of the Mexican people with the United States is demonstrated in many ways. Most noticeably, the Mexican media exhibit vast interest in Americans, their culture, and the policies of their government. In comparison, the American media give Mexico limited exposure. For every item about Mexico printed in American newspapers, scores of articles about the United States appear in Mexican dailies. For every Mexican movie shown in the United States, 100 American movies are shown to Mexican audiences. American television programs are widely viewed in Mexico, while Mexican television is little known in the United States.

The situation is changing, as this book will show. Recent developments have caused the American people to pay more attention to Mexican affairs. The United States "has lost control" of its southern border, the attorney general recently stated. The influx of illegal immigrants from Mexico is resulting in the "Hispanization" of the United States, according to some journalists. Meanwhile, Mexico has become an increasingly important customer of the United States, and Americans have added to their multi-billion-dollar investments in Mexico.

But it was the discovery of vast oil reserves in southeastern Mexico that most stimulated Americans' interest in their neighbor nation. Mexico, long subject to American domination, found itself in possession of an "oil weapon" that allowed it not only to resist encroachment, but also to make demands of its own.

The present scope—and the complexity—of Mexican-American relations are briefly surveyed in the following "views across the border" extracted from recent Mexican and American publications. Collectively, they serve as an overview of the following chapters.

In the Beginning

Even before Mexicans and Americans came into contact with one another in the borderlands, they had formed negative impressions of each other inherited from their respective mother countries, Spain and England. Seventeenth-century

New Englanders such as Samuel Sewall and Cotton Mather, for example, who had little direct contact with Spain or Latin America, took a jaundiced view of Catholic Latin America, based largely on what they had read in literature from England. Sewall believed that Mexican culture was doomed to fall before a triumphant Protestantism. . . .

The Texas Revolution and the Mexican War cost Mexico half of her national territory, and Mexicans living in this lost territory became the first substantial groups of Mexican Americans. Years of bloodshed intensified existing prejudices into deep hatreds which lingered long after the fighting was forgotten, especially in Texas, where the most blood had been spilled.

—David J. Weber, *Foreigners in Their Native Land* (1973)

Neighbors in Spite of Themselves

They are two populous, resource-rich nations with virtually nothing in common except a 2,000-mile border. For decades, the United States has bullied and bruised Mexico, but now the two countries are trying to settle old differences—and to adjust to a new relationship. Mexico—the world's fourth largest oil producer, and the United States' third biggest trading partner—has become an increasingly self-confident and independent nation determined to establish itself as a leader in Latin America.

—John Brecher, Beth Nissen, and Jane Whitmore,
Newsweek (June 15, 1981)

Obvious geographic factors and economic and societal ties

3

*clothe our relationship with Mexico with a special importance.
Few economies and societies are so entangled as those of
the United States and Mexico. . . .*

*For the United States the major issue posed by the common
border is immigration. As one study described it: Illegal immigration links so many sensitive concerns in both countries
that it resembles a "lightning rod" for the entire bilateral
relationship. Discussions regarding this issue in either country
inevitably lead to discussions regarding controversial conditions in the other country.*
—Viron P. Vaky, "Hemispheric Relations," *Foreign Affairs*
(vol. 59, no. 3, 1981)

Many Facets, One Problem

*Senator Simpson said that 85 percent of those who immi-
grate into this country this year would be Spanish-speaking;
that 80 percent of the babies born in Los Angeles County
hospitals would be delivered by mothers who were illegal
aliens; and that Spanish-speaking immigrants were assimilat-
ing into the mainstream of society at a substantially slower
rate than past groups of immigrants.*

*If these patterns continued, he contended, they could lead
to a nation with two cultures and two languages. This division,
he said, could lead to serious economic and social divisions.*
—*The New York Times* (June 22, 1981)

*Mexico's leading expert on migration, Jorge Bustamante,
criticized President Reagan's immigration proposals today. . . . For more than 100 years, Dr. Bustamante said,
"Mexican labor has been defined and conceived by many*

4

employers as a natural resource of the Southwest. But Mexi-
can labor is not cheap by nature. It is made cheap by the
laws of the United States and the practices of employers. . . .
The United States needs the migrants as it needs energy.
But undocumented persons are not the same as barrels of
oil. They are human beings, they have rights."

—*The New York Times* (August 5, 1981)

Uncounted thousands of Spanish-speaking aliens who flee
to this country each year to escape the crushing poverty of
their homelands are being virtually enslaved, bought and sold
on sophisticated underground labor exchanges. They are
trucked around the country in consignments by self-described
labor contractors who deliver them to farmers and growers
for hundreds of dollars a head.

—*The New York Times* (October 19, 1980)

Smuggling in Both Directions

Eight of the ten lanes of the international bridge at El
Paso were closed yesterday by immigration authorities of the
United States to permit closer inspection of vehicles in an
effort to halt the traffic in narcotics across the border. More
than 120,000 vehicles of American tourists who had been
in Mexico during the weekend were delayed for hours.

—*Excélsior* (July 1, 1980)

Of the $4 million worth of television sets that were exported
from Laredo to Mexico in 1978, approximately $2.8 million
was from smuggled sales. More than half of the contraband
television sets went overland; the rest went by air. Flying

contraband into Mexico from Laredo necessitates only a willing pilot and a landing strip.

—Tom Miller, *On the Border* (1981)

New Aspects of Old Problems

Old strains and new frictions are threatening to splinter traditionally close ties between the United States and oil-wealthy but uneasy Mexico. . . . Adding to American concerns are the rising tensions generated by Mexico's internal difficulties—widespread poverty despite the nation's oil wealth, inflation, lagging farm production, and an explosive birthrate that will increase population from its present 68.2 million to more than 100 million in the year 2000.

—*U.S. News & World Report* (March 9, 1981)

President López Portillo told the American editors that between Mexico and the United States there must be great frankness; the ancient formula of diplomacy must be considered outmoded. Mexico—as a sensitive, historically wounded nation—demands respect from its powerful neighbor. Without that respect, a satisfactory relationship will be impossible to maintain.

—*El Sol de León* (June 27, 1980)

President Reagan may not be an expert in foreign affairs, but he does know Mexico. Privately, he regards it as the most delicate problem confronting American diplomacy—more so than the Soviet Union.

—Charles Maechling, Jr., "Mexico, the Latin Pivot,"
The New York Times (September 5, 1981)

6

*Developments of the past 15 years have led U.S. policymak-
ers to reevaluate relations with Mexico, as a top-secret Presidential Review Memorandum from the National Security
Council revealed in late 1978. The main issues of concern
amid Mexico's growing instability are energy, trade, migration, and relations affecting border communities. The Presidential Memorandum reported: "No decision of any
consequence on either side of the border can have purely
domestic or purely foreign repercussions. Migration and economics are increasingly linking the politics of the U.S. and
Mexico, and not only in the Southwest border communities."*
—Peter Baird and Ed McCaughan, *Beyond the Border*
(1979)

*There are no isolated problems [in U.S.-Mexican rela-
tions]. Everything is part of everything else.*
—President José López Portillo (1977)

Past, Present, and Future

"Without considerable knowledge of the past, the present
is impossible to understand; without thought for the future,
the present has little purpose."
—According to Robert R. Parsons

The preceding observation is reflected in the organization
and content of this book. Attention is paid to current problems that affect day-to-day relations between Mexico and
the United States, and that occasionally produce a crisis.
To explain how these problems developed, Mexican history
is reviewed, with particular reference to the influence the

7

United States has exerted in the affairs of its neighbor republic. This background provides an explanation for current attitudes that Mexicans and Americans display in dealing with one another at the personal, as well as at the governmental, level.

Since geography and economics, as well as history, have made Mexico and the United States partners, however unwilling, current and future modes of resolving their differences are explored.

1

The Illegals

Juan García lay in the shadow of a pile of driftwood and looked across the river at the forbidden land. He had watched the shore all day, noting the plane that had flown low over the scrubby trees, wheeled when it was almost out of sight, and returned upstream. And through an opening in the underbrush, he had observed the patrol car as it went back and forth along the road that paralleled the river. . . . The Americans were working hard to keep him out of their country.

The sun sank behind him. As daylight merged into darkness, moving objects became hard to see. The time had come for him to cross the river. He took the compass from his pocket and put it into the bottom of the plastic bag he was carrying. Then he pulled off his boots, wrapped them in his clothes after he undressed, and stuffed everything into the bag.

He waded into the river as far as he could keep his footing. Having put the sack between his teeth, he eased into the current. When he reached the other side, he lay in an eddy and listened for man-made sounds. He dressed quickly, then studied the compass before it was completely dark.

While swimming, he had noticed an opening in the thicket that separated the river from the road. He avoided it, not wanting to leave tracks for some sharp-eyed American to discover in the morning. He pushed through the reeds, trying not to trample them. When he reached the road that ran alongside the river, he jumped over the dusty shoulder onto the asphalt. He ran along the road toward his objective until he heard a car in the distance. Once again he jumped over the shoulder of the road. So far, he had left no trail for a pursuer to pick up.

After easing his way down the embankment on the far side of the road, he pushed through thorny trees for several miles. He found a sheltered spot, struck a match, and checked his compass. In his own country, he could travel with the stars to guide him; here he depended on the strange little object that he had learned to use. The knowledge that he was on the course he had set made him forget how tired he was. He had a long way to go, and the danger of being caught had not lessened.

The sky was paling in the east. It was time to hide from the patrol. By resting all day, he could push himself hard that night. The next day he could reach his objective—

the railroad that connected Laredo with San Antonio.

*   *   *

It was Juan García's third attempt to elude the Border Patrol. He had made the first attempt in the company of four men he had met in Nuevo Laredo, on the Mexican side of the Rio Grande. When the night freight from Monterrey changed engines before it crossed the bridge, Juan and his friends crawled into a car that had sides but no roof. The train crossed the Rio Grande and passed through Laredo. Then it stopped. Suddenly, Juan saw a powerful light shining above him and heard a powerful voice commanding him to come from his hiding place. The Border Patrol officers took Juan and the other captives to a detention center, recorded their names, and questioned them briefly. When the officers found that it was their prisoners' first attempt to cross the border, they loaded Juan García and his friends into a van, drove them across the river, and released them in the plaza where they had met.

A smuggler of aliens, popularly known as a coyote, observed the conclusion of yet another failed attempt to elude the Border Patrol. The coyote approached his countrymen and offered his assistance. He claimed to have helped hundreds of illegals cross into the United States. He knew every feature of the river and of the land on either side. More important, he knew the Border Patrol's routine and all the means it used to trap unwary Mexicans: radio-equipped jeeps, planes and helicopters, and hearing devices that were planted for unsuspecting illegals to activate.

For a price, the smuggler offered to show Juan and his

friends how to get to San Antonio, where work was plentiful. He would take them across the river in his boat and guide them through the area where La Migra, as he called the Border Patrol, watched most closely. He offered a further service. He pulled a Texas road map from his pocket and showed his prospective clients where they were and where they wanted to go. With the help of the magic instrument that he would provide, his countrymen would not get lost. The coyote held a cheap compass in his hand and showed how it worked.

It was the compass that persuaded Juan García to part with so much of his precious money. He could read, unlike the others, and he saw the possibilities of what the coyote was offering. He asked the smuggler many questions, not only about the map and compass, but also about La Migra and how it trapped Mexicans after they had crossed the border.

That afternoon the coyote put the five men in his car and took them to his rowboat. Shortly after sunset, the Border Patrol left the opposite shore unguarded for a while. The smuggler rowed his passengers to the other side of the river, put them ashore, and hid his boat. He took his charges across the road into a canebrake. They hid there until the patrol car passed. Led by the coyote, the party then emerged from the reeds and walked several miles through the mesquite trees.

When the party reached a pasture, the smuggler took leave of his clients. As he shook hands with each man in turn, he assured them that if they followed his instructions they would reach San Antonio without trouble from La Migra.

What the coyote did not tell Juan García and his friends was just how far it was to San Antonio. Never having seen a map before, they had no idea how to estimate distance. Nor could they know that to reach heaven they would have to cross hell—150 miles of hot sand and thorny brush, where rattlesnakes were a lesser danger than the Border Patrol, and ranchers had been known to shoot trespassing Mexicans.

After walking for four cool nights and four blazing days, Juan and his friends were weak from lack of food, and almost crazed for water. Despite the coyote's warning that La Migra paid particular attention to irrigation ditches, the travelers found the water irresistible. To reach the ditch, they had to cross a dusty road that ran alongside it. Having drunk their fill, the five men found the nearest cover and fell asleep.

They were still napping when a Border Patrol jeep passed along the road. The driver noticed footprints, got out to examine them, and then radioed the pilot of the patrolling plane to help him find five wetbacks.

The captives were brought before the same officer who had dealt with them a few days before. This time he threatened them with jail. But instead of carrying out his threat, he had the famished men provided with food and water. Then, along with many other migrants, they were put into a bus that carried them far into Mexico before they were released.

If Juan García had been deprived of his map and compass, he would have returned to his wretched village a defeated man. He would have been forced to admit that he was not the equal of his brother, who had made it to San Antonio the year before, had found work, and had sent Juan money

A FAILED ATTEMPT. Every day of the year, several thousand Mexican citizens illegally enter the United States. The majority of them manage to elude the Border Patrol. Of those apprehended, some are jailed on charges of smuggling narcotics or for other criminal offenses, but most are sent back to Mexico.

Wide World Photos

to help him across the Rio Grande. But the map and compass provided the incentive to make a third attempt to reach his goal.

He parted company with his friends. They had proved a hindrance. One man could go where five could not; one man would interest La Migra far less than a group. This time, he applied what he had learned on the previous attempts. He walked along the riverbank until Laredo was out of sight. After swimming across the river, he struck out across country toward the place where the Border Patrol inspected the night freight to San Antonio.

Several days later, he came within sight of the tracks.

He found an abandoned corral where ranchers had penned cattle that were to be loaded on the train, and all day he lay under a rotting shed and listened to the trains passing in both directions. Twilight came, and then the darkness that he needed. He left his hiding place and walked toward the tracks. The approaching train shook the earth and sent a shiver up his spine. The locomotive slowed to a stop and the patrol appeared, with searchlights. He heard the Americans shout to one another when they caught a Mexican. He felt sorry for the captive, and resolved not to join him at the detention center.

La Migra moved from the engine toward the caboose. Just before the patrol got that far, Juan ran toward the waiting train. It jerked, then began to move. He caught the ladder of a likely-looking car and pulled himself up the side. As the train gathered speed, he dropped onto the contents of the car—metal pellets. They might get hot when the sun struck them, but long before that happened, he expected to be in San Antonio, where his brother was waiting for him with a job. He stretched out on his newfound bed and listened to the clicking of the wheels.

*   *   *

Every day of every year, thousands of Juan Garcías enter the United States from Mexico. These illegal immigrants are commonly referred to as "wetbacks," regardless of where or how they cross the border. This descriptive term has been used so widely that it no longer carries a derogatory meaning. The Juan Garcías who cross the border in such great numbers are more properly described as "undocu-

15

mented Mexicans"—a term that distinguishes them from Mexicans who enter the United States with visas or other entry permits issued by the American government.

Under the quota system established by the immigration laws of the United States, a maximum of 20,000 Mexicans may enter this country as prospective citizens in any given year. The competition for immigration visas is intense, and, with few exceptions, only Mexicans having a close relative who is an American citizen can hope to secure this type of document.

Mexican tourists, students, businessmen, and professionals may enter the United States with visas that indicate the duration of their stay and the conditions under which they are admitted. Violating the terms of the visa makes the person to whom it was issued subject to deportation. Overstaying the allotted time or securing employment in the United States are common violations of tourist and student visas.

Only the relatively affluent Mexican enters the United States with a visa. The great majority of those who cross the border are undocumented. Like Juan García, they attempt to elude the Border Patrol, establish residence in the United States, and remain there without detection. It is these undocumented immigrants who so trouble relations between the United Mexican States and the United States of America.

For obvious reasons, the number of Juan Garcías who enter the United States in a given year is a subject of speculation rather than a statistic. Most estimates made by experts on immigration are based upon the number of undocumented Mexicans who are arrested in a given year. In each of the last three years, the United States Immigration and Naturalization Service has apprehended more than a million illegal aliens, the majority of them Mexican citizens. A number of Border Patrol officials have stated that for every undocumented Mexican whom they apprehend, several succeed in entering the United States. If such statements are correct, then several million immigrants manage to cross illegally each year.

Such estimates must by treated with caution. For one thing, many undocumented Mexicans are apprehended several times in the course of a year—as in the case of Juan García—before they make a successful crossing. Other would-be immigrants are apprehended one or more times and never succeed in entering the United States. On the other hand, some undocumented aliens cross into the United States and return to Mexico the same year.

Although authorities on Mexican-American immigration differ as to the number of undocumented aliens who enter the United States in a given year, they agree that the number would be impressive if it could be ascertained. In fact, one expert believes that this illegal shift of population is the largest peacetime migration from one nation to another in the history of the world.

Moreover, the number of undocumented Mexicans who succeed in entering the United States is increasing, according to veteran Border Patrol officers. Authorities on immigration from the academic world support this opinion with their statements and published research. At a recent seminar sponsored by two prestigious research centers—El Colegio de Mexico and the Brookings Institution—the Mexican and

American experts in attendance generally agreed that illegal immigration to the United States is on the increase.

When so many people move illegally across a national boundary, problems are created for the "sending" nation as well as for the "receiving" nation. As a matter of fact, one of the gravest problems now facing the United States is the necessity of dealing with this influx of economically and socially disadvantaged Mexican citizens, few of whom speak English. Excluding these undocumented aliens, who are driven by powerful forces that are described in the following chapter, would be a difficult undertaking even if the international boundary were easily guarded. But the Mexican-American border is not only one of the longest international boundaries in the world—it is almost 2,000 miles long—it is also one of the most difficult to patrol.

The boundary crosses the North American continent from the Gulf of Mexico to the Pacific Ocean. For approximately half that distance the Rio Grande separates Mexico and the United States. Except during rare periods of heavy rainfall, or when water is released from dams that impound the Rio Grande and its tributaries, the river may be crossed by swimming a short distance. Frequently, an illegal immigrant may simply wade from Mexico to the United States.

From El Paso to San Diego, the international boundary crosses a desert, and there are no natural barriers to separate one country from the other. The relentless heat, the absence of water, and the rugged terrain discourage daytime desert crossings, but conditions are more favorable at night, when nature is kinder and the Border Patrol less effective.

The placement of cities along the Mexican-American border also facilitates illegal immigration. American and Mexi-

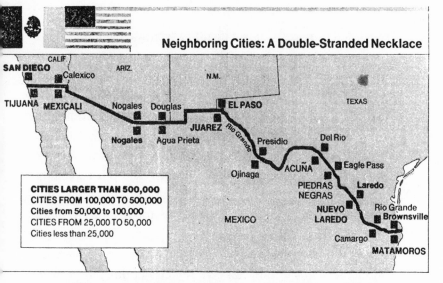

Neighboring Cities: A Double-Stranded Necklace

CITIES LARGER THAN 500,000
CITIES FROM 100,000 TO 500,000
Cities from 50,000 to 100,000
CITIES FROM 25,000 TO 50,000
Cities less than 25,000

POWERFUL ATTRACTIONS. Cities along the Mexican-American border are among the fastest-growing urban centers in the world. Drawn by employment opportunities north of the border, a growing number of Mexican citizens enter the United States illegally each year.

Copyright © 1979 by the New York Times Company. Reprinted by permission

can cities are paired: Brownsville and Matamoros, Laredo and Nuevo Laredo, Eagle Pass and Piedras Negras, El Paso and Juárez. Although the twin cities are separated by an international boundary, each pair actually forms one metropolitan district. Many permanent residents of the Mexican cities have permits that allow them to work or to shop on the American side of the border.

Along the international boundary from El Paso to San Diego, not even a river separates a Mexican town or city from its twin across the border. Since the cities are not

19

separated physically, it is difficult to separate them for immigration purposes. Tijuana, Mexico (population 850,000), and San Diego, California (population 800,000), are the largest of the paired cities along the international boundary. These two cities are of particular importance to immigration officials, because the border crossing between Tijuana and San Ysidro, a suburb of San Diego, is the busiest port of entry in the world. Thousands of cars, trucks, and other vehicles cross in each direction throughout the day and night, and at certain hours traffic may back up for a mile or more on both sides of the border.

When traffic peaks at this key border crossing, American immigration inspectors can give vehicles nothing more than a cursory examination, unless the vehicles are of a very suspicious character. At such times, coyotes take advantage of harassed immigration inspectors to smuggle their human cargo into the United States. To lessen the possibility of detection, they change vehicles and drivers frequently. Coyotes may even send radio-equipped cars ahead of the vehicles they are using to transport undocumented aliens across the border. Once a coyote's scout reports that conditions are favorable, a motor home, horse trailer, moving van, or other vehicle loaded with undocumented aliens will move past the checkpoint.

Undocumented aliens who cannot afford to pay a smuggler for identification (such as a forged birth certificate or Social Security card) and for transportation across the border may settle for expert guidance through the "no-man's-land" between Tijuana and San Diego. A more daring person may try it alone. The terrain invites such attempts but makes them hazardous. Hills, deep gullies, dry streambeds, drainage canals, and storm sewers offer protection for an undocumented Mexican who is willing to take chances. Even the multi-million-dollar chain-link fence that marks the international boundary for several miles has not proved a major obstacle. This once-formidable barrier has been tunneled under, cut through, and broken down at various points.

Newspaper reporters sometimes refer to the Tijuana–San Diego area as "the combat zone." More undocumented Mexicans attempt to cross into the United States at this point than at any other place along the border. The Border Patrol responds by making its greatest effort to halt illegal immigration at this point. The resulting conflict sometimes does resemble warfare. At first glance, the contesting forces seem unequal. According to the mayor of Tijuana, on any given day 250,000 of his countrymen are in the Mexican metropolis making plans to cross into the United States. Meanwhile, hundreds of coyotes, some of them working in cooperation with American employers, are arranging to smuggle their clients across the border.

Smuggling aliens to the United States has become big business. Immigration officials say that in the last five years the traffic in smuggled aliens has tripled. Since the coyote may charge an undocumented Mexican $300 for transportation to Denver and $500 for passage to Chicago, smuggling is very profitable—even more profitable than smuggling narcotics into the United States. The well-organized smuggling rings that operate out of El Paso and San Diego may move 500 undocumented aliens in a week, grossing $150,000 or

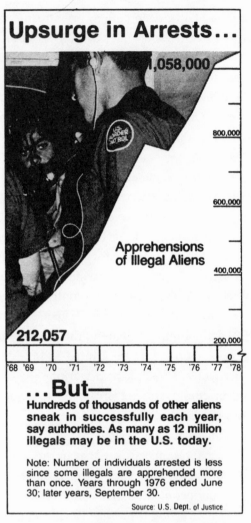

Upsurge in Arrests...

1,058,000

800,000

600,000

Apprehensions
of Illegal Aliens

400,000

212,057

200,000

0

'68 '69 '70 '71 '72 '73 '74 '75 '76 '77 '78

...But—

**Hundreds of thousands of other aliens
sneak in successfully each year,
say authorities. As many as 12 million
illegals may be in the U.S. today.**

Note: Number of individuals arrested is less
since some illegals are apprehended more
than once. Years through 1976 ended June
30; later years, September 30.

Source: U.S. Dept. of Justice

A CRUCIAL PROBLEM. Since the majority of illegal immigrants
who enter the United States come from Mexico, they are a major
source of friction in Mexican-American relations.

Reprinted from U.S. News & World Report, *Copyright* © *Jan.
29, 1979, U.S. News & World Report, Inc.*

more. Most operations are on a smaller scale, and they may involve American coyotes as well as Mexicans. (Several wives of U.S. Marines stationed at Camp Pendleton, California, were recently tried and convicted for transporting undocumented aliens from Tijuana to Los Angeles. The American women took the illegal immigrants through the Marine base to avoid the Border Patrol checkpoint at San Clemente.)

*   *   *

Ranged against the powerful force that hundreds of coyotes and hundreds of thousands of undocumented Mexicans represent is the Border Patrol, a division of the United States Immigration and Naturalization Service. The Border Patrol is responsible for controlling the movement of aliens along the Mexican border, the Canadian border, and along the Gulf Coast. In recent years, the Border Patrol has had an authorized strength of approximately 3,000 positions, most of them allocated to the Mexican border. The agency rarely has its full complement of officers, and since the Border Patrol operates on eight-hour shifts, only 350 officers are usually on duty at any one time along the 2,000-mile Mexican boundary. This is fewer than the normal force of policemen assigned to protect the U.S. Capitol and its office buildings, which occupy an area of about 100 acres.

To compensate for its limited personnel, the Border Patrol uses sophisticated devices to help it apprehend undocumented aliens. During the day, its patrol cars and planes are linked by radio telephone. At night, its helicopters can flood a large area with their searchlights, and infrared seeing devices "can spot a jackrabbit three miles away." Sensors that were developed during the Vietnam War are placed at likely crossing points. When activated by body heat or by vibration, these devices report movement that has escaped detection by the human ear and eye. Armed with the information provided by such equipment, Border Patrol officers round up undocumented aliens who would otherwise succeed in crossing into the United States. In one recent sweep, 50 Border Patrol officers surprised some 400 undocumented Mexicans on a levee of the Tijuana River that projects into the United States. Striking in two columns, and using tear gas and helicopters equipped with infrared spotlights, the Border Patrol apprehended the entire group of aliens.

Immigration authorities make a special effort to arrest coyotes, because they commit a criminal offense each time they bring an undocumented alien into the United States. The Border Patrol maintains checkpoints beyond the principal border crossings. Suspicious vehicles may be stopped and searched. When undocumented aliens are found in the cars, vans, and trucks used by smugglers, the vehicle may be confiscated—a procedure that discourages small-time operators. But large smuggling rings are not deterred by such seizures. They do not hesitate to sacrifice drivers and vehicles, because their profits cover such losses.

Pressure builds along the border as hundreds of thousands of undocumented Mexicans, intent upon entering the United States, face the relatively few immigration officers who are responsible for keeping them out. All too frequently, violence ensues. Sometimes the violence is limited to attacks on Border Patrol vehicles by rock-throwing Mexicans. But, when goaded, Border Patrol officers may respond with violence of their own. Thus two officers of the Border Patrol were found guilty in federal court of having led what the U.S. district attorney described as a "vigilante group" that inflicted beatings on Mexican aliens who crossed the border in the San Diego area.

Border Patrol officers are very rarely charged with misusing their authority; on the other hand, undocumented aliens who succeed in crossing into the United States are often mistreated by private parties. At several points along the border, criminals of Mexican descent prey upon illegal immigrants as they try to get their bearings in the United States. And ranchers on the American side of the border are sometimes charged with abusing undocumented Mexicans who trespass. For example, two prominent Arizona ranchers were recently tried for robbing and torturing three undocumented Mexicans whom they had captured at gunpoint.

Illegal immigrants suffer some of the worst abuses at the hands of the smugglers to whom they have entrusted their lives. If a coyote who is leading his clients through the famous storm sewers of Tijuana–San Ysidro discovers that his operation has been detected, he will abandon his charges and make his escape. And undocumented Mexicans who are being transported by a smuggler sometimes have a far more hazardous passage than those who go on foot. Police officers in Houston recently stopped a beer truck for a traffic violation. Locked in the truck, they found 55 undocumented Mexicans. The aliens told the policemen that they had been without food and water for two days. More recently, a car caught fire near a border checkpoint and the driver fled.

Screaming inside the car attracted the attention of an immigration officer. When he succeeded in opening the trunk of the car, he found two undocumented Mexicans who had burned to death.

The troubles of undocumented immigrants are not over after they cross the border and establish residence in the United States. The Immigration and Naturalization Service may have failed to bar such aliens, but it maintains an interest in them as long as they remain in the United States. The surprise raids that immigration officers make on places where undocumented aliens live and work result in the expulsion of thousands of Mexican citizens each year. Unscrupulous employers, in order to avoid paying their undocumented workers, may report them to the immigration authorities, or the local police may notify the Immigration Service of the presence of persons whom they believe to be illegal aliens. Even a personal enemy may denounce an undocumented alien to the immigration authorities. In short, as long as undocumented Mexicans remain in the United States, they are oppressed by fear and uncertainty.

Accounts of the frantic efforts of undocumented Mexicans to establish residence in the United States are usually harrowing—and sometimes they are tragic. Such reports raise an obvious question in our minds. Why do hundreds of thousands of Mexicans—who are notably attached to their country, and even more notably devoted to their families— suffer incredible hardship and often jeopardize their lives in trying to enter a country that makes a strenuous effort to keep them out?

2

Criminals or Refugees?

If their present rates of growth are maintained, the population of Sweden will double in 1,386 years; the population of France will double in 198 years; and the population of the United States will double in 99 years. However, the population of Mexico will double in 22 years.

This projection from the International Statistical Institute draws attention to the explosive growth rate of the Mexican population. Census returns provide more specific information. In 1910, Mexico had a population of 15.2 million and an annual growth rate of 1.1 percent; by 1950, the population had increased to 25.8 million, and the annual growth rate had risen to 2.8 percent. Preliminary returns issued by the Mexican census bureau in 1980 gave the national population as approximately 68 million, and the rate of growth as 3.26 percent. In recent years, Mexico has had an annual net increase in population greater than that of Canada and the United States combined, even though its total population is now roughly one-fourth that of its two neighbors. The population of Mexico is expected to pass the 100 million mark before the end of this century. In short, at a time when many nations are approaching zero population growth, Mexico has a rapidly expanding population.

The dramatic growth of the Mexican population is due almost entirely to natural increase. Few people have migrated to Mexico from other parts of the world. The vast majority of its citizens are descendants of the native Indians and the Spaniards who conquered them. In this respect, Mexico differs from the United States, which has absorbed so many Europeans, Africans, and Asiatics that it is sometimes referred to as a nation of immigrants.

Since 1940, the Mexican death rate has fallen sharply, due to improved health care, sanitation, and nutrition—but the Mexican birthrate has remained one of the highest in the world. Deeply ingrained in the Mexican culture is the acceptance of large families as the norm. For centuries, Mexican men have believed that fathering many children is a necessary proof of masculinity. For centuries, Mexican women have been taught to play a submissive role as wives and mothers. Unquestioning compliance with such standards precludes limiting the size of one's family. Indeed, to do so would diminish self-respect and invite the disapproval of the community.

The deep-seated belief that mankind's proper role is to

multiply has been supported in Mexico by both church and state. Most Mexicans are Roman Catholic. The Church has always opposed birth control by means of abortion and the use of contraceptives, and the views of the Church were shared by the Mexican government until recent years. Thus, when President Echeverría was inaugurated in 1970, he denounced efforts to limit population with the use of contraceptives. "We need to populate our country," he said. "We do not want to control our population."

But as the Mexican economy faltered and the population explosion jeopardized President Echeverría's ambitious plans to improve living conditions, he made a radical change in official policy. To prevent population growth from forestalling economic growth, the all-powerful president endorsed family planning as public policy. Under his direction, the Mexican congress revised the Law of Population in 1973 to permit the government to institute a program to stabilize population growth. A year later, a guarantee that all persons have the right to decide on the number and spacing of their children was incorporated into the Mexican constitution. In the meantime, the Roman Catholic bishops endorsed a family-planning program based upon Church doctrine. The change in policy was explained by the bishops in terms of "the very sad and excruciating emergency for most Mexican families: the population explosion."

Mexican leaders who regarded runaway population growth as the gravest problem facing their nation welcomed changes in the policies of the church and state. Nevertheless, some critics on both sides of the Rio Grande view the present efforts to bring Mexican population growth under control as halfhearted at best. In the opinion of such critics, the Mexican government is highly authoritarian, and so it has the power to persuade, or at least pressure, the people of the country to have fewer children. But they think that a more comprehensive and sustained educational campaign, conducted through the schools, radio and television, and the press; the use of tax incentives and penalties; and the distribution of free contraceptives are means that the Mexican government might use in curbing population growth. More outspoken critics of present policy go so far as to say that until Mexican authorities display a willingness to deal realistically with their basic problem, they should not expect the United States to accept impoverished aliens for whom their own government does not provide.

But there are population experts who challenge the explanation for the explosive increase in the Mexican population outlined above. They contend that prosperity and security encourage *low* population growth, as in Sweden, while poverty and insecurity are incentives for large families, as in Mexico. The noted ecologist Barry Commoner summarized this argument when he said, "It is poverty that causes overpopulation, not the other way around." According to this point of view, the surest way for the Mexican government to curb population growth is *not* to employ the methods mentioned above, but to raise the standard of living of its impoverished citizens.

The trouble is that even if the Mexican government were to make an all-out effort to end the population explosion, it would not be able to achieve the desired result for some

RURAL POVERTY, A CAUSE OF MIGRATION. The impoverished people of rural Mexico create social, economic, and political problems when they migrate to cities in their own country or enter the United States illegally in search of work.

Inter-American Development Bank

years. In the meantime, the population crisis requires massive short-term efforts on the part of government officials, business leaders, and other decision-makers. If the Mexican population doubles between now and the end of the century, as expected, the food supply will have to be doubled. For every school in operation at present, another will have to be erected by the year 2000; the number of job opportunities will have to be doubled, and public agencies will have to double their services. In other words, in order to keep the Mexican living standard even at the present unacceptable level, the production of goods and services will have to expand at the same rate as the population. The possibility that this will happen seems remote.

* * *

The enormous expansion of the Mexican population in itself creates conditions that impel migration within the country, and emigration to the United States. Changes in technology and government policy likewise bring about shifts in population. Of all the population shifts that have occurred, none has had a more profound effect (not only in Mexico, but also in the United States) than the exodus of people from rural Mexico. The character of the land, government policy, and technological changes have forced millions of Mexicans to leave their native farms and villages in recent years.

More Mexicans could remain on the land if nature had endowed their country with greater natural advantages. Most of the land in Mexico is too dry, too wet, or too mountainous to cultivate. Approximately one acre in six is arable, and one acre in twelve is actually cultivated. The total area in Mexico now under cultivation is roughly equal to the acreage planted to crops in the state of Iowa. The limited soil resources of Mexico must be kept in mind when considering the need to increase food production.

Mexico has been handicapped not only because of the character of the land, but also because the ownership of the land has been a matter of dispute ever since the nation became independent. While the Indians dominated what is now Mexico, land was held in common—that is, the land belonged to the tribe rather than to individual owners. The

Spanish conquerors substituted private ownership of land for community ownership. The Spanish monarch gave enormous tracts of land to the captains who had conquered an empire for him, and much land was set aside as an endowment for the Roman Catholic Church.

As the centuries passed, land ownership became concentrated in fewer and fewer hands. On the eve of the Mexican Revolution (1910), approximately 97 percent of all land was held by 830 owners, including prelates serving as agents for the Church. Two percent of the land was the property of some 500,000 Mexicans, while the remaining 1 percent was all that remained in community ownership.

Landless Mexicans finally rebelled against the system that had reduced them to virtual slavery. The military phase of the Mexican Revolution lasted ten years and cost an estimated one million lives. A large part of the country was devastated, and most of the great landowners, including the Church, were stripped of their property.

During the course of the revolution, a new constitution was adopted. The redistribution of land was one of its major provisions. The constitution of 1917 revived the system of collective ownership by authorizing *ejidos,* or agricultural villages surrounded by land that belonged to the community as a whole. Small plots were also given to individuals.

Despite the prohibitions of the constitution, a new class of landowners came into existence—Mexicans who, through political influence or outright bribery, acquired extensive tracts of land. The power of this new, privileged class was challenged by several presidents, notably Lázaro Cárdenas, who expropriated and redistributed thousands of acres of illegally acquired land. In redistributing land, Cárdenas and several of the presidents who followed him temporarily placated the peasants, who were dangerously restive, having been denied what they had fought for during the revolution.

In the period 1915–1965, the Mexican government distributed millions of acres of land to small farmers. But in the same period, the government built vast irrigation projects in the arid northwestern part of Mexico. This activity served to strengthen the landowning class and to increase the number of landless, migrant workers. By bringing water to the desert, the Mexican government made possible the system of agriculture that had proved highly successful in adjoining California and Arizona. Favored individuals and corporations acquired extensive tracts of land, often with loans from government banks. Using water supplied at low cost from reservoirs built by the government, the landowners developed the type of operation known in the United States as "agribusiness." Such enterprises were large-scale, highly mechanized, and dependent upon the use of fertilizers, insecticides, and other chemicals. Expert management was required, not only to produce good crops of cotton, sugar, and vegetables, but also to market those products in Mexico and the United States.

The extensive use of machinery relieved agribusiness from dependence upon unskilled labor most of the year, but at harvest time large numbers of migrant workers were needed. Landless Mexicans followed the harvest, and they were unemployed much of the year unless they crossed the border and found work in the United States.

The famous "Green Revolution," which began in Mexico in 1943 and spread to other parts of the world, also favored large-scale agriculture and penalized small farmers. Working under the sponsorship of the Mexican government and the Rockefeller Foundation, scientists developed varieties of food grains that doubled or tripled production from a given acre. But the high-yielding cereal grains had to be grown on the best land, preferably under irrigation, and they required the application of fertilizers and insecticides. So the Green Revolution favored the large, well-financed operator. Contrary to Mexican law, which limits an owner to 250 acres of irrigated land, individuals who had political influence acquired much larger tracts.

PEOPLE OF MEXICO

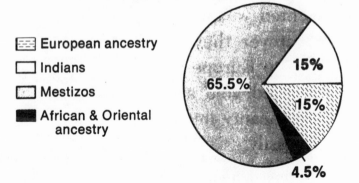

- European ancestry
- Indians
- Mestizos
- African & Oriental ancestry

65.5%
15%
15%
4.5%

MEXICANS AND AMERICANS COMPARED. Of the people now living in the United States, approximately one in ten is foreign born. In contrast, about one in a hundred Mexicans is foreign born. The great majority of Americans are descendants of immigrants who came to the United States from many parts of Europe, Africa, and Asia. In contrast, the majority of Mexicans are mestizos—descendants of native Indians and the Spaniards who conquered them.   *From* In a Race with Time, *by E. B. Fincher. Reprinted by permission of Macmillan Publishing Co., Inc.*

As its name indicates, the Green Revolution produced striking results. Between 1950 and 1970, wheat production in Mexico increased 800 percent, the corn harvest increased 250 percent, and the bean crop almost doubled. Mexico had surplus grain to export. But then production leveled off. Population growth overtook agricultural production, and Mexico was forced to import grain.

In favoring agribusiness and neglecting small farmers, the Mexican government made the country more dependent on the United States. The principal crops of the irrigated farms of northwestern Mexico—tomatoes, strawberries, and winter vegetables—were produced largely for export to the United States. Periodically, American competitors in Texas and Florida demanded restrictions on the importation of Mexican produce, and some Mexicans began to insist that instead of growing luxury foods for American consumption, the irrigated farms of the northwest should be growing corn and beans—foods that are the basis of the Mexican diet.

*   *   *

Rural Mexicans reacted in various ways to the changes that were taking place in agriculture. Some were angered by the failure of their government to provide credit, technical assistance, and other aid to small farmers, while it did provide these to large landowners. And when the government awarded lands that had been reclaimed from the desert to large operators, rather than to small farmers, it antagonized rural Mexicans, who wanted public officials to stick to their promise to break up large holdings.

Some peasant leaders were not content to criticize their government for failing to complete the land reforms begun by the Mexican Revolution. In the 1970s, militant leaders aroused landless farmers and set up the Independent Peasant Front and other activist organizations. When the government did not accede to their demands to redistribute land, armed peasants occupied large agricultural properties in many parts of Mexico. President Echeverría ordered the army to eject peasants from some of the land that they had occupied, and in other cases he ended the occupation by having the peasant leaders jailed. But armed peasants continued to occupy land that they claimed properly belonged to them.

To the surprise of the great landowners and the landless farmers alike, President Echeverría made a dramatic about-face in the closing weeks of his administration. The president expropriated more than 200,000 acres of northwestern farmland. Almost half of the acreage was irrigated land that belonged to some of the largest property owners in Mexico. The land taken by the president was promptly given to 8,000 peasants.

But landless Mexicans who thought that Echeverría's 1976 redistribution was the beginning of a new era in land reform were soon disappointed. Shortly after a new president, José López Portillo (1976–1982), came to office, he made a break with the past. He announced that there was no land left for distribution to peasants, and that jobs would have to be created in agriculture for landless farmers. In effect, President López Portillo admitted that the land reforms begun by the Mexican Revolution had come to an end.

*   *   *

The number of peasants who tried to force the government to redistribute land was small when compared with the total rural population. Subsistence farmers continued to eke out a living from their tiny plots of land without showing outward signs of rebellion. They produced no surplus food—but they did produce surplus people. Since the land could not support the subsistence farmer's large family, some of his children were forced to join the ranks of migrant workers, or to move to the city in search of employment.

The exodus to the cities brought about a radical redistribution of the population. In 1910, the year the Mexican Revolution began, approximately 70 percent of the population was rural. By 1980, the rural population had declined to about 40 percent of the total. According to the National Urban Development Plan, only 20 percent of the Mexican population will be classified as rural when the census is taken in the year 2000.

As the rural population has declined, the urban population has increased in a striking manner. In 1910, there were few urban centers in Mexico, and the largest of them, Mexico City, had a population of only 500,000. By 1980, Mexico City and its suburbs had a population exceeding that of the entire nation in 1910. A study recently made by the United Nations showed that Mexico City, with a metropolitan population of more than 15 million, was outranked only by New York and Tokyo among the cities of the world.

By the year 2000, Mexico City is expected to have a metropolitan population of 31 million, which will make it by far the largest city in the world. The National Urban Development Plan predicts that by the turn of the century, 37 percent of the Mexican people will live in three metropolitan districts: Mexico City, Guadalajara, and Monterrey.

The rapid shift of population from rural to urban Mexico had far-reaching effects on every phase of national life. Indirectly, it affected relations with the United States. The municipal governments of the largest cities could not cope with the influx of people from farms and villages. Housing, water mains, sewers, and electric lighting could not be provided fast enough for the hordes of new residents. But the lack of such facilities did not deter rural people from pouring into the already overcrowded cities. When nothing else was available, the newcomers took possession of vacant land on the outskirts of the cities and erected huts from scrap lumber, cardboard boxes, tin cans, and other materials they found in garbage dumps. In a surprisingly short time, Mexican cities were ringed with shantytowns where thousands of people lived without piped water, sewers, or electricity. In these "belts of misery," newly arrived peasants lived under conditions almost as primitive as those they had endured in rural Mexico.

The influx of people made cities almost unmanageable. Public transportation facilities were so overtaxed that breakdowns were frequent. A seeming avalanche of rural children overwhelmed urban schools. Open sewers spread disease. Since there were far more job-seekers than there were jobs, cities had high concentrations of the unemployed. These

DISADVANTAGED AGRICULTURE. Most of Mexico is unsuited for farming because of its arid climate and rugged surface. Rural people who cannot make a living on the land migrate to Mexican cities or to the United States. *Inter-American Development Bank*

jobless people posed a threat to law and order, because their hopeless condition made them prone to violence.

Changes in the geographical distribution of the Mexican people created grave problems for the government officials who were responsible for providing public services. And changes in the age distribution of the Mexican people created equally serious problems. The high birthrate gave Mexico a youthful population compared with the populations of the United States and Western Europe. In 1980, approximately half of the people in the United States were under 30 years of age, and half were older than that. In Mexico, approximately half of the people were under the age of 15, and half were older than that. To put it another way, the median age of the people of Mexico was much lower than the median age of the American people.

When compared with the United States, Mexico had a disproportionate number of school-age children. As a consequence, the Mexican government had an extra burden in caring for its youthful population. Educational facilities had to be enlarged to cope with a steadily expanding school-age population. An ever larger outlay of public funds was required to provide essential health services, such as mass immunization against childhood diseases. And as it struggled to supply educational facilities and health care, the Mexican government was also called upon to help provide young people with jobs when they finished school. In each of these efforts, the Mexican government was far from successful. As a matter of fact, most young Mexicans, like their elders, have not fared well in recent years.

*   *   *

Millions of Mexicans live under such miserable conditions that they move from one part of their country to another or enter the United States illegally in an effort to better their lot in life. *"¡Sal si puedes!"*—Spanish for "Get out if you can!"—is a common expression that reduces to a few words the feeling of despair that countless Mexicans have when they look about them. In *The Children of Sanchez,* Oscar Lewis described the lives of these impoverished Mexicans. Conditions have not changed much since Lewis published his famous book in 1961.

For instance, the present mortality rate for Mexican preschool-age children is about 12 times as high as that for the same age group in the United States. An explanation for this high infant death rate was recently offered by the director of the Faculty of Nutrition at the University of Veracruz. He stated that almost one-third of all Mexican infants suffered from malnutrition, and that the percentage of deaths attributable to that cause was rising. But malnutrition is not restricted to the preschool population. President López Portillo noted in 1980 that over 40 percent of the Mexican people were chronically undernourished.

Despite the efforts of the government to provide every child with an education, only 56 percent of the school-age population was actually in school in 1980. Mexico still has a high rate of illiteracy: about one out of six Mexicans cannot read or write.

Mexico has become highly industrialized in recent years. The rapid expansion of its economy since 1940 has been referred to as the "miracle" of Mexico. Of the Latin American nations, only Brazil rivals Mexico in the organization and output of its textile factories, steel mills, oil refineries, sulfur and petrochemical plants, and automobile industry. According to the World Bank, Mexico now has the 19th largest economy in the world. But despite its remarkable expansion in recent years, Mexican industry has not provided enough jobs for would-be workers. The labor force grows at the rate of about 700,000 persons a year. As presently organized, the Mexican economy cannot create that many new jobs. The result is that only about half of the Mexican working force is fully employed, according to Saul Trejo Reyes, economic adviser to the president of Mexico.

The other half is unemployed or partly employed, or manages to live just at the subsistence level by working on the family farm or in the family business.

A number of economists and political scientists say that "Get out if you can!" does not need to be the advice that many parents give their children. Millions of Mexicans would not have to live in abject poverty if the wealth produced in their country were more evenly shared. Redistribution of income would raise the living standard of many Mexicans, according to economists. As it is, few countries in the world have a more inequitable distribution of income than Mexico has. The privileged 10 percent of the population receives 45 percent of the national income. The deprived 40 percent of the Mexican population receives 10 percent of the national income.

A recent study showed that the present inequality in Mexicans' income is comparable with that in 1910. That was the year the Mexican Revolution began—the revolution that was to bring an end to inequality. There are critics on both sides of the Rio Grande who maintain that if the redistribution of wealth promised by the revolution were finally brought about, Mexicans could live comfortably in their own country, instead of being forced to migrate to the United States in search of work.

*   *   *

When the U.S. House of Representatives considered a bill to increase the manpower of the Border Patrol not long ago, one congressman objected to an appropriation for that purpose. He argued that even if there were enough Border

Patrol officers so that they could stand shoulder to shoulder all along the Mexican-American boundary, they would not be able to halt the flow of illegal immigrants into the United States. The representative's statement called attention to the tremendous pressure exerted by hundreds of thousands of Mexicans made desperate by the socioeconomic conditions just described in this chapter. In a sense, the representative acknowledged that undocumented Mexicans violated American law because they had no alternative.

The concept of the undocumented migrant as an economic refugee finds support in a comprehensive, ongoing study being made by a staff headed by Jorge Bustamante of El Colegio de Mexico with funds provided by the Mexican government. A composite picture of this economic refugee was derived from 10,000 interviews conducted with undocumented Mexicans immediately after their release by the United States immigration authorities, who had apprehended them.

The profile of the typical undocumented Mexican describes a person living at the margin of subsistence, with no possessions to sell when facing a crisis brought about by a drought, a flood, a death in the family, or the loss of a job. When confronted by such a catastrophe, this Mexican concludes that there is no alternative to migration to the United States.

An American specialist on migration, Wayne Cornelius of the University of California at San Diego, gives a somewhat more detailed picture of the undocumented Mexican. Drawing on his own research and that of other investigators, Cornelius reports that a majority of the migrants are males between 22 and 30 years of age. About half of them are married, but few are accompanied by their wives. Of the women who enter the United States illegally, most are members of families that emigrate together, or they are the dependents of men who have already established residence in the United States. (Other researchers report that the number of unmarried women migrating to the United States is on the rise. Most of them remain near the border, whereas male migrants are likely to move into the interior of the United States.)

The Cornelius profile depicts the typical undocumented Mexican as rural in background, and as having no more than three years of schooling. This typical migrant comes from the lower income level of his or her community, but is *not* a member of one of the poorest families. The poorest Mexicans cannot borrow money to pay for their trip, and ordinarily they do not have relatives in the United States who can finance them.

The typical undocumented Mexican comes from the central plateau—an area where migration to the United States has become a traditional "way out." The chances are that other members of the migrant's family and many of his or her acquaintances have worked across the border. In fact, in some rural communities, at least half of all adult males have worked in the United States. The undocumented Mexican who plans to migrate usually receives advice (and sometimes financial assistance) in his or her community; and, once across the border, the migrant can depend upon friends and relatives for assistance in finding a job and establishing residence.

The Bustamante and Cornelius studies reduce to a personal level the economic, social, and political forces that drive millions of Mexicans into the United States, despite the hazards of emigration. Such studies also call attention to the "pull" forces from the American side of the border that reinforce the "push" forces exerted on the Mexican side.

3

The Magnet

"The United States is now the fourth largest Spanish-speaking nation in the world."

"Los Angeles is second only to Mexico City in the number of its Mexican inhabitants."

"One out of four Texans is of Mexican descent."

"The Bureau of the Census reports that since 1970, the number of persons of Hispanic descent living in the United States has increased 33 percent—while the nation's overall population has increased only 6.1 percent and the black population has increased 11 percent."

"By the turn of the century, the Hispanic population of the United States, three-fifths of it Mexican Americans, will surge past black Americans to become our largest minority."

These statements from recent reports on population changes underline some of the long-range effects of Mexican migration to the United States. For the most part, such studies focus attention on the undocumented Mexicans who now are entering the United States in record numbers. The current immigration scene arouses interest because it is marked by high drama: a rich, powerful country uses sophisticated methods to exclude the impoverished but ambitious citizens of a weaker nation, many of whom are brought across the border by smuggling rings. Their interest in undocumented Mexicans having been aroused, a number of Americans have studied the "pull" factors that have induced millions of undocumented Mexicans to enter the United States.

In some parts of the world, lofty mountains, broad rivers, and impassable deserts hinder the movement of people from one country to another. But migration from Mexico to the United States is easy, geographically speaking. No mountains block passage from south to north, and no rivers seriously impede migrants. Highways and railroads have made the desert safe to cross. Since most undocumented Mexicans have someplace in the southwestern United States as their objective, they are actually just moving from one section of a geographic region to another. This geographic region consists of the northern part of Mexico and the southwestern United States. As far as topography and climate are concerned, the area that lies on either side of the Mexican-American border is a distinct region; the international boundary is a purely artificial division. The undocumented Mexican who plans to enter the southwestern United States is encouraged by the fact that the country to which he or she is going looks remarkably like the country he or she will be leaving behind. Where physical environment is concerned, migrants feel very much at home once they are across the border.

Moreover, migrants will find themselves in a fairly familiar social environment, because many elements of Mexican culture have been preserved in the Southwest. That part of the United States has been under American domination for less than 150 years, while it was under Spanish and Mexican domination for more than 300 years. Spanish-speaking people have left their imprint on what is now Texas, New Mexico, Arizona, and California. Consider the names of some of the major rivers of the Southwest: Colorado, Pecos, Rio Grande, Brazos, and Nueces; of some of its major mountain ranges: San Juan, Sangre de Cristo, and Guadalupe; and of some of its major cities: Los Angeles, San Diego, Santa Fe, El Paso, and San Antonio.

Descendants of the Spaniards who named those rivers, mountains, and cities continue to live in the Southwest. They have perpetuated the culture brought to the area by the soldiers, friars, and settlers who accompanied Coronado and other Spanish explorers of the 16th century. Other Spanish-speaking Americans who live in the southwestern United States trace their ancestry to Mexicans who migrated there after their country won its independence from Spain in the

49

early 19th century. The Mexican settlers who came to the Southwest before the United States annexed it put their stamp on the region, just as the Spaniards did. The Mexican influence shows in the architecture, cuisine, music, and dance of the Southwest. The English-speaking people of the region enrich their speech with Mexican expressions, and enjoy amusements borrowed from the neighboring nation.

The highly visible evidence of Mexican culture in the Southwest makes the area attractive to undocumented Mexicans. The presence of great numbers of Spanish-speaking people in that part of the United States makes it easier for the undocumented Mexican to elude American immigration authorities. And with the arrival of each new immigrant from Mexico, the Spanish-speaking population of the United States is enlarged, and its culture is reinforced.

*   *   *

The physical and cultural environment of the Southwest has facilitated migration from Mexico, but the chief attraction that the United States has always had for the Mexican migrant is economic. Mexican migration, both legal and illegal, has resulted primarily from American offers of employment. For more than a century, Southwestern farmers, railroad builders, and factory owners have valued Mexico as a source of cheap labor. Openly or covertly, they have induced Mexicans to cross the border. Through the years, the federal government has abetted the recruitment of Mexican workers during periods when the national economy is expanding.

The United States deprived Mexico of half of its territory

UNACCEPTABLE LIVING STANDARD. Although privileged Mexicans shop in ultra-modern supermarkets and otherwise enjoy a high living standard, the scene above reflects the lives of less advantaged Mexicans. To escape poverty, millions of Mexican citizens have sought employment in the United States.

Inter-American Development Bank

as the price of defeat in the war waged between 1846 and 1848. With the discovery of gold in California shortly thereafter, Americans began to pour into the former Mexican territory. The Civil War interrupted the settlement of the Southwest, but when the conflict ended, the area developed rapidly. Railroads were extended from the Great Plains to the Pacific. Silver and copper mines were developed, and ranchers assembled vast tracts of land for grazing their sheep and cattle. Stretches of the Southwestern desert were converted to citrus groves, vineyards, and truck farms as dams were thrown across rivers to impound water for irrigation.

The rapid development of the resources of the Southwest created a demand for labor. When the domestic supply was short, or when American workers rejected the wages and conditions of employment offered them, Mexicans were recruited. Beginning in the 1880s, employers sent their agents across the border to induce Mexicans to come to the Southwest to work on the railroads or in the mines. At the same time, Texas cotton growers, California truck farmers, and Colorado beet sugar producers recruited Mexicans for the "stoop" labor that their large-scale operations required. By 1900, the use of Mexican migrant labor was considered essential for the profitable operation of the vineyards, truck farms, and citrus groves of the Southwest.

And government policy favored the migration of Mexican workers. They were exempted from the payment of certain taxes, and prohibitions against the use of contract labor were not applied to them. When the immigration authorities apprehended Mexicans who had crossed the border illegally, their admission could be legalized if an American employer would pay for a visa.

While Mexican workers were being pulled to the United States by the prospects of employment, they were being pushed from their own country by an upheaval there. The revolution that began in 1910 almost ruined the country. Rival generals marched and countermarched their armies from one end of Mexico to the other, leaving paths of destruction in their wake. Communications and transportation broke down, business came to a standstill, and fields were left unplanted wherever the conflict spread. Having been driven from their homes, countless Mexicans sought refuge outside the war zone. Some of these refugees from the revolution looked to the United States as both a haven and a place of employment.

The outbreak of World War I affected Mexican refugees by increasing the demand for their labor. As soon as the United States entered the conflict, President Wilson called on American farmers to increase production to meet wartime needs. But it was difficult to comply with the president's request when thousands of young men were leaving the farms for the army. Herbert Hoover, who headed the U.S. Food Administration during the war, regarded the use of Mexican labor as the answer to the American manpower shortage. Hoover asked the Department of Labor to relax its restriction that limited Mexican migrants to agricultural work. "It is hardly necessary to say that these men are needed for various other kinds of work in Texas and New Mexico, and this restriction first of all should be disposed of." Hoover also objected to any regulation that would discourage a Mexican migrant worker from remaining in the United States. "We do not *want* him to return to Mexico," Hoover said. After recommending several other changes that would encourage more Mexican workers to come to the United States, Hoover argued that "we need every bit of labor that we can get, and we need it badly . . . and we will need it for years to come."

But Herbert Hoover took a different view of Mexican labor after he became president in 1929. During his administration, the economic depression that afflicted American agriculture after World War I spread to industry. Factories shut down, mines curtailed production, storekeepers went out of business, and bankers foreclosed mortgages. Millions of men and women were thrown out of work. The Great Depression quickly affected Mexicans who had been attracted to the United States when the economy was booming. Unemployed Americans accused Mexican workers of holding jobs that properly belonged to the native-born. Hostility was first directed at Mexicans who worked on Southwestern farms. But migrants who had found employment in Midwestern factories aroused even more resentment, because many of them were doing skilled, well-paid work.

As unemployment increased throughout the United States, national organizations such as the American Federation of Labor and the American Legion demanded that the federal government deport Mexican workers in order to create jobs for native-born Americans. But, for the most part, the campaign to expel Mexican migrants was waged at the state and local level. Officials who administered welfare programs claimed that money should not be spent on jobless Mexicans, because it was needed for jobless Americans. The fact that foreigners were on relief sometimes provoked local officials to the point where they demanded the expulsion of *all* Mexicans who lived in their communities.

In some instances, local officials threatened to deprive Mexican citizens of welfare payments, and thus forced unwanted aliens to return to their country "voluntarily." In several California towns, Mexican aliens were provided with railroad tickets and were escorted to the border to make sure that they left the United States. The governor of Michigan worked out a plan for the "repatriation" of thousands of Mexican citizens who had been working in the factories of Detroit and other Michigan cities. With the cooperation of their own government, trainloads of Mexicans were accompanied to the border by state law-enforcement officers. There they boarded trains provided by the Mexican government.

In their book, *Mexican Workers in the United States,* George and Martha Kiser estimate that almost 500,000 Mexican citizens returned to their country during the depression of 1929–1939. Some went because they could no longer find work in the United States. Others were forced to leave because of pressure brought by state and local officials. Some were frightened into leaving by vigilante groups of hostile Americans. Among those forced to leave with the aliens were many naturalized American citizens of Mexican birth, American wives of Mexicans, and children who had automatically acquired American citizenship when they were born to Mexican parents in the United States. The Spanish surnames of these Americans made them Mexicans in the eyes of persons determined to oust alien workers.

The forced "repatriation" of Mexican citizens caused grave hardship, and their expulsion brought bitter protests from Mexican editors and government officials. A number of American newspapers and magazines condemned the "repatriation" campaign in equally severe terms. The whole episode was described as yet another example of the ill-treatment that Mexican workers so frequently suffered in the United States.

* * *

"When the United States sneezes, Mexico catches cold" is an expression used to illustrate Mexican sensitivity to the American economy. As long as the United States is prosperous, Mexico benefits. When a depression develops in the United States, its effect is soon felt south of the border. In fact, the movement of Mexican migrant workers across the border is a good index of economic conditions in the United States. That correlation was emphasized in the 1940s. The last of the "repatriated" Mexicans had scarcely been sent across the border before American employers and public officials wanted them to return. The outbreak of World War II in 1939 brought an end to unemployment in the United States as the democratic nations of Europe turned to this country for the food and weapons they needed to resist Hitler and his allies. American farmers and manufacturers increased production to meet wartime needs.

When the United States entered World War II, the call for maximum output became more urgent. But a manpower shortage developed on American farms, thus jeopardizing the war effort. Farmers complained that the war industries paid such high wages that rural workers were streaming to the cities. Agribusiness in the Southwest was particularly hard-hit, and large landowners called for the recruitment of Mexican labor to supply their needs.

Under pressure from farm organizations, Congress passed laws that paved the way for the importation of millions of Mexican laborers. A program that came to be called the *bracero* program, after the Mexican word for laborer, was set up. The agreement that went into effect in 1942 reflected the reaction of the Mexican government to the treatment its citizens had received during the depression of 1929–1939. The Mexican government insisted on labor contracts that would protect its citizens from the kinds of abuses they had suffered in the past. The contracts specified the rate of pay, the hours of work, and the type of housing and health services to be provided for each worker. The *bracero* was to be protected against discrimination, and was to be supplied with round-trip transportation so that he might return to Mexico when his contract expired. To further guarantee that its citizens would be treated fairly, the Mexican government insisted that the government of the United States serve as the official employer of the *braceros*. Private employers would contract with their own government for the needed labor.

The agreement reached by Mexico and the United States also contained provisions designed to protect American labor. *Braceros* were to be used only where there was a labor shortage, and they would be confined to agricultural work. They had to be paid the prevailing wage for such employment so as not to undercut American workers.

The original *bracero* program operated between 1942 and 1947. From 1947 to 1964, the program continued on a less formal basis. (For example, American employers were allowed to contract directly for migrant workers; they no longer had to go through their government.) During the various phases of the *bracero* program, more than four million seasonal workers were brought to the United States under contract.

The effects of the *bracero* program—which many Americans regarded as a temporary, wartime measure—may be seen today. Millions of "invited" Mexican workers became familiar with the United States and its employment possibilities. The pay that they received enabled them to improve the living conditions of their families in Mexico. When their contracts expired and they returned to Mexico, the *braceros* had a powerful incentive to return to the United States as "uninvited" workers. Making the prospect that he would return more likely was the former *bracero*'s ability to cross the border on his own and to reestablish himself in familiar territory.

Even before the *bracero* program ended, the number of undocumented Mexicans who crossed the border had begun to rise. The presence of thousands of undocumented workers threatened to undermine the system of contract labor. Illegal migrants would work for less pay than those under contract, and they were in no position to complain about the conditions under which they lived.

MILLIONS OF MIGRANTS
by decade

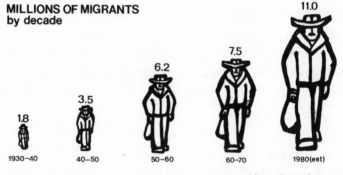

| 1.8 | 3.5 | 6.2 | 7.5 | 11.0 |
| 1930–40 | 40–50 | 50–60 | 60–70 | 1980(est) |

Source: Mexican Government

ROOTLESS MEXICANS. The population explosion and the expansion of large-scale mechanized agriculture have caused a rapid increase in the number of migrants seeking employment in Mexican urban centers or in the United States.

From Beyond the Border, *by Peter Baird and Ed McCaughan.*
Reprinted by permission, North American Congress on Latin America

To discourage the flow of illegal migrants, Congress strengthened the laws against transporting and concealing illegal aliens. The Border Patrol stepped up its efforts to apprehend undocumented Mexicans—a campaign that culminated in "Operation Wetback," a dragnet-style roundup of illegal aliens carried out with military precision in 1954. For the next decade, the number of undocumented Mexicans who were apprehended remained at a fairly low level.

Although the Mexican government wanted to continue the *bracero* program, strong opposition eventually developed in the United States. American labor leaders called on the federal government to end the importation of contract workers, because their employment made it difficult to organize native-born workers and to secure an acceptable wage scale for them. Civil rights leaders urged Congress to end the *bracero* program, charging that migrant workers were so exploited that they should be regarded as slave labor. First President Kennedy and then President Johnson opposed the continuation of a system that they regarded as a violation of the principles of the Great Society. Congress reflected American public opinion when it ended the *bracero* program over the objections of the Mexican government.

With the termination of the *bracero* program, a major barrier to illegal immigration was removed. Many Mexicans felt that they had no choice but to migrate illegally. After 1964, there was a sharp increase in the number of undocumented Mexicans who entered the United States. The apprehension of more than a million illegal immigrants in successive years did not deter other millions of Mexicans from making border crossings.

In explaining the inability of the Border Patrol to prevent illegal immigration, authorities on population problems pointed out that while federal law made it illegal for an undocumented Mexican to enter the United States, federal law did *not* make it illegal for an American employer to hire such a person. This discrepancy promoted illegal immigration by encouraging undocumented Mexicans to believe that they would find employment if they succeeded in eluding the Border Patrol.

It was the Nobel laureate economist Milton Friedman who bluntly stated the reason why American employers and public officials actually encouraged undocumented Mexicans to cross the border. His article in the October, 1978, *Saturday Evening Post* argued that Mexican immigration to the United States is a good thing for both countries. But, Friedman said, "It's only a good thing so long as it's illegal. That's an interesting paradox to think about. Make it legal and it's no good. Why? Because so long as it's illegal the people who come in do not qualify for welfare, they don't qualify for social security, they don't qualify for all the other myriads of benefits that we pour from our left pocket into our right pocket. So long as they don't qualify, they migrate to jobs. They take jobs that most residents of this country are unwilling to take."

Underlying the undocumented Mexican's willingness to make a hazardous border crossing, and to accept work that most Americans are said to disdain, is a grim economic fact. As noted in a recent editorial in *The New York Times,* nowhere else in the world are so many poor people (Mexicans) living so close to so many rich people (Americans).

Although Mexico is now a rapidly developing country, its per capita income is about one-seventh that of the United States. As an influence on illegal immigration, the differential between the Mexican and the American wage scale is of even greater consequence than the difference in per capita income. Since the average wage that the undocumented Mexican currently receives in the United States is approximately *five times* the minimum wage paid in Mexico City, he or she has a powerful incentive to cross the border in search of work.

"U.S. Inundated by Wetbacks"

"Rising Tide of Illegal Aliens"

*"Illegal Immigrants Threaten
American Institutions"*

Headlines such as these are indicative of the fears aroused by illegal immigration. In the absence of reliable statistics on illegal aliens in the United States, many Americans believe that the number is alarming. And since undocumented Mexicans constitute the majority of all illegal aliens living in the United States, attention has focused on them.

Undocumented Mexicans must elude immigration authorities in order to enter the United States, and for that reason the number who cross the border is unknown. As noted in an earlier chapter, estimates of the number of successful crossings are made on the basis of the number of illegal entrants who are apprehended and either jailed or returned to Mexico. If the number of undocumented Mexicans who enter the United States in a given year is no more than an approximation, then the number of illegal aliens living in this country in a given year is also a conjecture, rather than a verifiable figure.

As one would expect, estimates of the number of illegal aliens living in the United States vary widely. In the last ten years, the Immigration and Naturalization Service has given figures ranging from 8 million to 12 million. Analysts of the Social Security Administration recently estimated that there were 4 million undocumented aliens in the United States. A study prepared by the Bureau of the Census in 1980 estimated that the number of illegal immigrants residing in the United States was between 3.5 million and 6 million. This study concluded that illegal Mexican aliens living in the United States "almost certainly" numbered fewer than 3 million and "possibly only 1.5 to 2.5 million."

Figures released by the Mexican government in 1980 set the number of its citizens living illegally in the United States even lower than the U.S. Bureau of the Census. The Mexican study was based on detailed interviews conducted in 58,000 households in different parts of the country. From the resulting data, population experts estimated that the number of Mexicans living illegally in the United States varied from 480,000 to 1.2 million, depending upon the season of the year.

Approximations such as these indicate that the majority of illegal immigrants living in the United States are Mexican citizens. Although thousands of Asiatics; people from the

Caribbean countries; and natives of Colombia, Ecuador, and Peru enter the United States illegally each year, undocumented Mexicans attract greater attention because they constitute a conspicuous minority in a number of states.

What such estimates do not reveal is the unique character of illegal immigration from Mexico. It remained for Mexican and American researchers, such as Jorge Bustamante of El Colegio de Mexico and Wayne Cornelius of the University of California at San Diego, to call attention to an important difference between undocumented Mexicans and their counterparts from other parts of the world. Illegal immigrants from Asia, the Caribbean nations, Central America and South America must make a radical change in their lives when they come to the United States. They almost always cross an ocean in their long, expensive journey. Like the European immigrants who came to America in the 1800s, most illegal aliens from countries other than Mexico plan to remain in the United States for a long period, if not permanently.

In contrast, undocumented Mexicans tend to be transients. The proximity of the United States and the ease of entering it illegally enable the undocumented Mexican to come and go almost at will. Extensive interviewing conducted by Wayne Cornelius and his staff revealed that undocumented Mexicans who remain in the United States for short periods outnumber those who settle permanently by a ratio of eight to one. Almost half of those interviewed had gone to the United States and returned to Mexico at least twice. The Cornelius study indicated that most undocumented Mexicans returned to their country when their seasonal work ended, or when they had accumulated enough money to meet the need that had caused them to migrate. The short-term character of much of the migration between Mexico and the United States has notable effects on both sides of the border, as the following chapter will show.

4

Migrant Labor:
Pro and Con

Before the coyote hid Elena and the other women behind
the cartons, he warned them to keep quiet all the way,
but above all whenever the van stopped. The first test would
be the border crossing, where La Migra probably would
let them pass without a search. If they stopped a second
time, it meant that they had been waved down at the checkpoint between San Diego and Los Angeles. Then there might
be trouble, because La Migra would look inside the van.

Well, they had been stopped a second time, which meant
that they were in danger. Elena heard the driver using English, so she knew that he was talking to La Migra. Although
it was pitch-black behind the boxes, she closed her eyes
and steeled her muscles. She expected to be dragged from

her hiding place. If they didn't put her in jail, they would send her back to Mexico. Worse, she would lose the money she had paid the coyote. She had borrowed that money from her godfather, and it was all he had.

Elena heard the door of the van open, and saw a shaft of light shift from one place to another. When La Migra moved a carton, her heart skipped a beat. Then the door slammed shut and the van began to move. As soon as she knew that La Migra had let them pass, Elena crossed herself and said a prayer.

After that, they traveled very fast until they turned from the highway onto a street. Before long they stopped at a place where someone removed the boxes and the other women got out of the van. Then the driver took Elena to the address that she had given him.

Once she was with her aunt and all her cousins, Elena forgot that she was in a strange country, without her children, without money, and without a job. Her relatives in Los Angeles would look after her until she earned money for her keep and to send home. The house had so many people living in it that she wondered where she would sleep. The question was soon answered: she would share her cousin's bed, even if it wasn't meant for two grown women.

She had hoped to spend at least one day recovering from her hard trip, but that was not what her aunt had in mind. In order to make ends meet, everyone in the family had to work, had to work every day. There was a job waiting for Elena in a garment factory where one of her cousins knew the boss. All she needed was a Social Security card, a sort of work permit that Americans required when they hired someone. Her aunt put the precious card in Elena's hand and explained that it belonged to an in-law who was glad to help out a member of the family.

As Elena's aunt had predicted, the American who owned the shop hardly glanced at the Social Security card that she showed him. In his halting Spanish, he asked if she knew how to run a sewing machine. When she said that she did, he had her make a man's shirt from the pieces that the cutter had stacked on a table for distribution to the operators.

The boss hired her after explaining the hours of work and the rate of pay. Elena made a quick calculation. She would make more money in a day than she had made all week in the little shop where she had worked in Mexico. But she soon discovered that she would have to work hard for everything she got. The boss was a slave driver. She worked at top speed, determined to prove how fast she was, but the cutter kept adding to the cloth beside her machine. She could never get to the bottom of the pile. And every time she looked up from the shirt she was making, the owner or his foreman was watching her. By afternoon, her eyes burned and her back ached. The noise made by all those sewing machines bothered her, but not as much as the heat. The windows were all closed, so the air seemed as dead as it was hot. She was glad when the other women began to cover their machines and she knew that it was time to quit.

That night she had little taste for food, although her aunt urged her to eat, and she found it hard to sleep on half of the narrow bed. The only relief was the thought of the money that she would send home at the end of the week.

For the first few days she had no mind for anything but

her machine. After that, she began to notice her fellow workers. There were 30 of them, all Mexicans like herself—or so she thought at first. There were a few girls who smiled at the way she talked and made fun of the clothes she wore. Those stylish ones proved to be Americans, even though they spoke Spanish. "Chicanas" they called themselves, to indicate that they were different from Mexicans like Elena. It was obvious that they felt superior. Her aunt had warned her about such people. They might resent the fact that Elena had entered their country illegally, and yet was receiving as much pay as a citizen. Sometimes, Chicanas would tell La Migra about an illegal whom they disliked in order to get rid of her. That warning put Elena on guard and made her worry.

After La Migra raided a shop not far from hers and arrested several undocumented Mexicans, Elena was so apprehensive that she dreaded going to work. She heard other stories that added to the tension—among them a report that bosses sometimes turned Mexicans over to La Migra when they complained about their pay or hours of work. Much of the time she felt like a slave; at other times she felt like a criminal. But then she received a letter from her mother, telling about the children. She felt ashamed of herself, and proud that the money she sent to Mexico would provide a better life for her children than she had experienced at their age.

* * *

The account of Elena's first days in the United States emphasizes the marked effect that illegal immigration has

CHANGE OF EMPLOYMENT. Until recent years, most undocumented Mexican women employed in the United States worked as field hands or as servants in Southwestern homes. Today, such illegal aliens are chiefly employed in the garment industry or on factory assembly lines.

on the life of an individual Mexican. When thousands of Elenas cross the border in a given year, the impact on the "sending" nation—Mexico—and on the "receiving" nation—the United States—is no less profound.

The northward migration from Mexico has been likened to a safety valve. The population pressure caused by a high birthrate is relieved when a million or more Mexicans are absent from their country each year. By removing themselves from the competition for food, housing, and jobs, migrants lessen the possibility of an upheaval caused by their government's failure to provide many of its citizens with the basic necessities of life.

But undocumented workers who migrate to the United States do more than reduce the strain on Mexico's socioeconomic system. In most cases, the migrant's chief purpose in going to the United States is to earn money to send home. The total amount remitted in a given year can only be approximated, since the number of undocumented Mexicans in the United States is not known for certain. However, authorities on immigration have interviewed migrant workers in this country and in Mexico, and they estimate that undocumented Mexicans send their families approximately $2 billion each year.

Money sent home by undocumented Mexicans often represents the sole support of their families. In other cases, remittances from the United States supplement the family income and bring it above the subsistence level. In the case of rural Mexicans, money sent from the United States permits the recipients to remain in familiar surroundings; without this income they would be forced to seek employment in the already overcrowded cities. Remittances from the United States thus promote stability in the Mexican countryside.

When undocumented Mexicans return from the United States, they often bring new skills, acquired while working across the border, that they put to use in their own country. In addition, the returning migrant may bring money saved while he or she was in the United States; this money can buy tools, livestock, or other property that will help to improve the living standard of the migrant's family.

But it is not only Mexican families who benefit from the remittances of migrant workers. The Mexican government profits. Since Mexico buys more from the United States than it sells to the United States, there is always a trade deficit. Money remitted by Mexicans working in the United States helps to ease their country's balance-of-payments problem. (In 1980, Mexican exports to the United States totaled $9.7 billion. Imports from the United States totaled $12.1 billion. In other words, Mexico had a trade deficit of $2.4 billion.)

Mexico benefits from the migration of its citizens to the United States, but in some ways, Mexico is harmed. Hundreds of thousands of its able-bodied young people help to build the economy of the United States instead of working for the advancement of their own country. Moreover, the fact that so many of its citizens must seek employment in a foreign nation is a reflection on the Mexican government. The large-scale migration of its citizens clearly shows that the Mexican government has not been able to provide its people with the benefits described in the constitution and promised them by successive presidents.

*   *   *

The 1980 census showed that Los Angeles had overtaken Chicago as the second most populous city in the United States. *The New York Times* noted that "while few people dwelled on the matter, there was a pattern in the turn of events: Los Angeles, a city founded by Mexicans, appeared to have become the country's second largest city because of a renewed wave of immigration from Mexico." The wave of immigration to which *The Times* referred was primarily an influx of undocumented Mexicans, who were joining

American citizens of Mexican descent to form California's largest and fastest-growing minority.

Undocumented Mexicans ordinarily are regarded as an alien group more or less confined to the Southwest. California, Texas, Arizona, and New Mexico still attract more Mexican aliens than other states, but undocumented Mexicans now live in sizable numbers in many parts of the country. Chicago is the objective of great numbers of Mexicans who are smuggled into the United States; these illegal aliens make up a large part of the estimated 700,000 Spanish-speaking residents in the nation's third largest city. Another Midwestern metropolis, Kansas City, has an Hispanic community of 50,000, most of whom are illegal aliens from Mexico. In the South and East, most major cities have contingents of undocumented Mexicans who have traveled great distances in search of work.

Today, Mexican migrants not only travel farther afield than they formerly did—they also settle more often in cities than in rural areas. The change from rural to urban living reflects the growing tendency of undocumented Mexicans to find employment outside agriculture. The demand for low-paid agricultural workers has declined, but the demand for low-paid laborers in the service industries has increased. In many American cities, the restaurants, hotels, fast-food chains, and hospitals rely upon undocumented Mexicans to do the menial work. The construction industry employs thousands of unskilled and semiskilled Mexican migrants. Other migrants work in food-processing plants. Many undocumented Mexican women work as household servants throughout the Southwest, but increasingly they find employment in the garment industry and in assembly plants.

Some undocumented Mexicans hold white-collar jobs, but most of the Mexican migrants who are skilled laborers fall into the blue-collar category—they are carpenters, masons, upholsterers, and so forth. The great majority of the undocumented Mexicans now working in the United States are on the lowest rung of the labor ladder. In this respect, they resemble the immigrants of previous generations—such as the Irish and the Italians—who worked long hours for low pay when they first arrived in America.

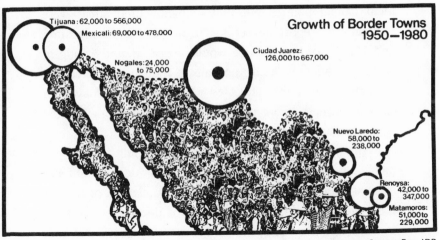

Source: Fox, IDB

POPULATION EXPLOSION. Mexican cities along the border have grown rapidly in recent years because of the regional industrialization program sponsored by the Mexican government. Having moved from the interior to the border, many Mexicans then illegally cross into the United States in search of work.

From Beyond the Border, *by Peter Baird and Ed McCaughan.*
Reprinted by permission, North American Congress on Latin America

Like earlier generations of immigrants, undocumented Mexicans are frequently exploited. An investigative team from the U.S. Department of Labor recently found that 60 percent of the employers it checked in Houston "were shortchanging alien workers by paying less than the Federal minimum wage, by not paying for overtime or by not compensating them fully for all hours worked." The chief of the Labor Department investigative team cited one case in which undocumented Mexican women were paid less than *half* the hourly wage prescribed by law for their work in a mail-order merchandising company. The Labor Department official pointed out that undocumented aliens were reluctant to report abuses for fear that the Immigration and Naturalization Service would deport them. Acting in behalf of undocumented Mexicans in the Houston area, the Department of Labor collected $350,000 in back pay from employers, and where possible returned the money to the workers who had been defrauded.

Civil rights leaders, both inside and outside the government, have attempted to end the exploitation of undocumented aliens by promoting stricter enforcement of present laws and by adding further legal protection. But the right to fair economic treatment is not the only protection that civil rights leaders want for undocumented aliens. In its September, 1980, report, the United States Commission on Civil Rights advocated changes in the immigration laws and in the methods used to enforce them. The commission singled out the raids conducted by immigration agents for particular criticism. In their pursuit of illegal aliens, federal agents often violate the rights of American citizens, according to the commission. For example, federal agents sometimes enter the homes of citizens without a court order, and question the occupants solely because they look Hispanic or speak Spanish. Moreover, many illegal aliens picked up by federal agents are deprived of the civil rights to which *all* people are entitled in a democracy such as the United States. The right to a fair hearing was emphasized by the commission.

An important federal court decision that involved the civil rights of undocumented Mexicans was handed down in July, 1980. The case involved a Texas law that barred the children of illegal aliens from attending public schools. Civil rights lawyers, with the support of the U.S. Department of Justice, brought suit against 17 school districts, charging that Texas had deprived as many as 100,000 children of their constitutional rights. The federal district court overturned the Texas law on the grounds that it violated the equal-protection clause of the Fourteenth Amendment.

The federal judge cited practical as well as constitutional reasons for setting aside the Texas law. Excluding alien children from school did them great personal harm, he said, and would prevent them from becoming part of American society. The judge reminded Texas lawmakers of the role that public schools have played in creating a united nation from numerous and diverse immigrant groups. According to the court, most of the children affected were already permanent residents of the United States. If denied an education, they would be so handicapped that the government would in the course of time have to provide them with some form of welfare. The ultimate cost of denying the children of illegal aliens an education would exceed the present cost of their schooling.

Texas authorities carried the case to the U.S. Court of Appeals for the Fifth Circuit. The appellate court upheld the ruling of the lower court. By the time the case was appealed to the U.S. Supreme Court (1981), President Reagan had assumed office, and a new attorney general represented the United States. As spokesman for the Reagan administration, Attorney General Smith told the Supreme Court in the brief he submitted that the federal government had no interest in the case—a statement that Texas officials interpreted as tacit support for their position. Attorney General Smith seemed to strengthen the Texas appeal when he pointed out that regardless of the outcome of the case pending before the Supreme Court, laws passed by Congress would continue to exclude illegal immigrants from receiving federally funded benefits such as Medicare, food stamps, unemployment compensation, and welfare.

On June 15, 1982, the United States Supreme Court upheld the decision of the Court of Appeals for the Fifth Circuit. The Supreme Court ruled, 5 to 4, that children who are illegal aliens have a constitutional right to a free public school education. The effect of the ruling was to require Texas and other states to provide illegal alien children with the same type of education provided children who are American citizens.

Immigrants have played a controversial role in American society ever since the United States became a nation. Arguments defending and decrying the use of alien labor that are made today sound very much like arguments made in the 18th and 19th centuries. In times of prosperity, the immigrant is welcomed. When economic conditions worsen, the employment of aliens becomes a political issue. And since undocumented Mexicans are not only aliens, but *illegal* aliens at that, their presence in great numbers stimulates an unusually sharp debate. Taking the "pro" side are certain economists who believe that illegal aliens play a necessary role in the United States. Almost all undocumented Mexicans who cross the border are young people who have cost the United States nothing in the way of expenditures for housing, education, health care, or other government services. The able-bodied immigrants have a powerful incentive to make good. For that reason they are willing to work longer, at lower wages and under less favorable conditions, than those acceptable to most Americans. Their fear of deportation not only makes undocumented Mexicans docile workers—it also discourages them from applying for such benefits as unemployment insurance, hospitalization, and welfare—which the native-born worker expects as a matter of course. In other words, some employers regard undocumented Mexicans as ideal workers.

A study recently made by the U.S. Department of Labor showed that three out of four illegal aliens paid federal income and Social Security withholding taxes, but that fewer than 3 percent had children in school, and that fewer than 2 percent received food stamps. The Department of Labor found that in San Diego, illegal aliens used an estimated $2 million worth of public services in the year surveyed, but paid approximately $49 million in taxes on the wages they earned. The Department of Labor study received sup-

77

port from research conducted by T. Paul Schultz, an economist and demographer at Yale University, and Julian L. Simon, an economist at the University of Illinois. Their 1980 study found that "the average immigrant is a remarkably good investment for taxpayers." Schultz and Simon also discovered that there was not much difference between legal and illegal immigrants in their economic progess in the United States. The Schultz–Simon study concluded that immigrants were "not heavily on welfare or unemployment compensation rolls, as the popular wisdom has it."

Employers who make use of migrant labor contend that Americans would pay more for many of the products that they eat, wear, or use if undocumented Mexicans were denied the right to work in the United States. And since illegal aliens are willing to do the menial labor that many native-born Americans have come to disdain, undocumented Mexicans help to maintain the life-style for which the United States has become famous.

As the United States approaches zero population growth, some business leaders and economists look to the future with uneasiness. Ever since the United States became a nation, it has had an expanding population and an expanding economy. The growth system that has made the United States the most productive nation in the history of the world will be weakened if the number of workers and consumers remains stationary or declines. In this sense, undocumented Mexicans now entering the United States are a benefit—they offset the declining birthrate of the "host" country. Like the previous influx of European immigrants, the present wave of undocumented Mexicans will assure the continued

"STOOP" LABOR. Although many undocumented Mexican men still harvest crops throughout the Southwest, the number of rural workers is dwindling. An increasing number of men who enter the United States illegally find work in the construction, service, and other urban industries. *Wide World Photos*

growth of the American economy.

Arguments that support illegal immigration do not go unchallenged. State and local officials may concede that the federal taxes paid by undocumented Mexicans exceed the cost of the federal services they receive. But state and local officials maintain that the situation is somewhat different at their level of government. Burdette Wright, an official of the Los Angeles county government, cited a recent study to show that illegal aliens are a burden on Los Angeles County taxpayers. According to the report, 6,000 undocumented Mexican women received maternity care in a county hospital during the year, and in that same year $13 million was spent on emergency medical treatment for undocumented Mexicans. The total cost of medical services provided Mexican aliens that year was $52 million—an expenditure financed by taxes paid by the U.S. citizens living in Los Angeles.

The Texas law that barred the children of undocumented aliens from attending public schools called attention to another burden imposed upon state and local governments. In defending the law in federal court, attorneys for the state of Texas stressed the cost of providing an education for thousands of children whose undocumented parents seldom pay property taxes—the taxes from which public schools are largely financed. "Besides," the Texans asked, "why should we pay for the education of alien children whose presence in our state is the result of lax law enforcement on the part of the federal government?"

A number of labor leaders, along with spokesmen for certain minority groups, believe that undocumented Mexicans deprive native-born citizens—particularly black Americans—of employment. Both labor leaders and spokesmen for black Americans contend that the people whom they represent do *not* refuse to do so-called menial work. It is a matter of pay and working conditions. If decent wages were paid for such work, jobs would be filled by the native-born. But employers will not pay a living wage to Americans as long as they can make a better profit by hiring undocumented Mexicans at rates below the federal minimum wage, and by working them under sweatshop conditions. Such illegal practices increase unemployment among American citizens, who cannot be intimidated into foregoing the wages and benefits due them.

Some employers not only exploit undocumented Mexicans to the detriment of black Americans and citizens of Mexican descent, but also use illegal aliens to prevent the formation of labor unions, and as "scabs" to break strikes. During the late 1960s and early 1970s, the strike of the United Farm Workers union, led by César Chávez, was prolonged by the growers' ability to use undocumented Mexicans to harvest their crops. Since a majority of the members of the farm workers' union were Americans of Mexican descent, the long, bitter strike created hostility to Mexican aliens, even though they belonged to the same ethnic group as the strikers.

The farm workers' strike illustrated the complex relationship between American citizens of Mexican ancestry and the undocumented Mexicans living in their midst. Mexican Americans, or Chicanos as many call themselves, have strong kinship, language, and cultural ties with Mexican aliens. However, Chicanos and undocumented Mexicans often compete for the same jobs. Since a Mexican alien is usually willing to work for less than a Chicano, he or she is likely to get the job.

Competition from undocumented Mexicans has changed the status of many Americans of Mexican ancestry. Vernon M. Briggs, an economist at the University of Texas, noted that both the 1950 and the 1960 censuses showed that the

Chicano was the least urbanized of the major ethnic groups in the Southwest. The 1970 census showed that Chicanos had become the *most* urbanized ethnic group in the Southwest. The Texas economist attributed the radical change to the displacement of Chicanos as rural workers by undocumented Mexicans. In Briggs's opinion, many Chicanos forced from the rural economy were unprepared for their new life in the urban labor market. "In this way, the illegal Mexican aliens have caused serious economic hardship and geographic dislocation to the Chicano labor force of the rural Southwest."

The economic competition between Chicanos and undocumented Mexicans was described by Joseph J. Jova, an American of Mexican descent who once served as United States ambassador to Mexico. Speaking at a Brookings Institution conference on migration problems in 1978, Jova reported that Chicano leaders who live near the border were very critical of U.S. immigration authorities for not "stemming the tide of illegal migrants." The former ambassador's observation was borne out by a survey made by Senator Lloyd Bentsen of Texas among his constituents with Spanish surnames. Eighty percent of those responding to the survey favored drastic measures to limit the flow of undocumented Mexicans across the border.

Relations between Chicanos and undocumented Mexicans are complicated by the fact that while an American of Mexican ancestry may regard aliens *in general* as a threat, a relative who crosses the border will be welcomed. And, while most undocumented Mexicans may intend to return to their native land, many eventually acquire American citizenship.

An undocumented Mexican becomes eligible to apply for naturalization papers if he or she marries an American citizen, or becomes the father or mother of a child born in the United States. Furthermore, great numbers of undocumented Mexicans may eventually become American citizens if Congress enacts proposed legislation that would permit the naturalization of illegal aliens who have lived in the United States for a certain number of years. Such a law would enhance the role that Americans of Mexican descent play in the affairs of their country. It would also have a significant effect on relations between the governments of the two nations involved.

5

The Chicanos

"When I was in school, the teachers beat me if I spoke Spanish. They wanted to remind me that I was an American. After school, my friends beat me if I spoke English. They wanted to remind me that I was a Mexican."

This boyhood memory of a present-day Mexican-American leader illustrates the divided allegiance that members of minority groups have felt through the years. But Mexican Americans have unique problems, because they belong to a minority group that differs from any other. Immigrants from the various European countries became members of minority groups when they voluntarily came to the United States and sought American citizenship. A black minority group was formed by individual Africans who were forcibly brought to the United States. Mexican Americans became a minority group when the area in which they lived was conquered by the United States.

Mexicans lived in what is now the western United States for 200 years before the first Americans reached that part of the continent. They became a minority group against their will when the United States deprived Mexico of half of its territory following the war of 1846–1848. The estimated 1,000 Mexicans who lived in what is now Arizona, the 5,000 who lived in what is now Texas, the 7,500 who lived in California, and the 60,000 who lived in New Mexico became Americans with the signing of a peace treaty, and not because they had any wish to become citizens of the United States.

The vast majority of the Mexican Americans now living in the United States are descendants of immigrants who came to this country after 1848. But even new arrivals from Mexico may feel that they have a special position in the United States because a large part of it once belonged to their native country. A blunt statement of that view was made by Obed López, a Mexican citizen who appeared before a committee of the U.S. House of Representatives that was considering immigration legislation in 1971. "We take the position that Mexicans as part of the native population of America have an inherent right to inhabit this territory. We propose that you recognize, in considering this legislation, the fact that Mexican land was taken by armed force. You have ignored the basic rights of Mexicans to live in the land while you opened your gates to the flood of European immigration. As long as this continues, the problem of illegal entry will persist."

Although Mexican Americans constitute one of the oldest ethnic groups in the United States, they have attracted relatively little attention until recent years. The 1954 Supreme Court decision that outlawed racially segregated public schools focused attention on Mexican Americans as well as on black Americans. Members of both minority groups had been forced to attend segregated public schools in many Southwestern communities.

During the 1960 presidential campaign, John F. Kennedy recognized Mexican Americans as a disadvantaged ethnic group and promised to improve their status if he was elected. Once in office, he proposed a number of bills that would aid Mexican Americans; these became law after his assassination. When President Johnson succeeded John F. Kennedy, he pushed through Congress legislation that affected both Mexican Americans and black Americans. As civil rights laws began to take effect, and as the "war on poverty" got under way, an awareness of the plight of Mexican Americans developed in the United States.

Between 1965 and 1970, a series of dramatic events made the activities of Mexican Americans front-page news. César Chávez organized the Mexican-American farm workers of California into a union, and demanded higher wages and better working conditions for its members. When the grape growers refused to bargain with the union, Chávez led the farm workers in a strike. *La Huelga*—"The Strike"—became a rallying point for Mexican Americans, first in California and then throughout the Southwest. The strike also received support from thousands of people in other parts of the nation. Sympathetic Americans boycotted non-union grapes, thus helping the farm workers to bring the growers to the negotiating table after five bitter years. During those five years, César Chávez became a nationally known figure.

César Chávez always insisted upon nonviolence, but Reies López Tijerina of New Mexico used force in an effort to achieve his objective, which was the return of land that he alleged had been stolen from the Spanish-speaking people of New Mexico after the war of 1846–1848. In 1967, Tijerina and his followers marched on the state capital with a petition for redress of injustice. Later, the group occupied part of a national forest and seized a county courthouse. When Tijerina was tried and jailed for his activities, he focused national attention on the grievances of the Mexican Americans of his state.

In the late 1960s and early 1970s, the Vietnam War caused unrest among Mexican Americans, as it did among other aroused citizens. Mexican-American troops sustained a higher percentage of casualties than the armed forces as a whole. Mexican-American leaders, charging that the disproportionate number of casualties was the result of discrimination in the drafting and disposition of troops, organized protests in several Southwestern cities. During the largest of these demonstrations, held in Los Angeles, violence erupted, and the leading Mexican-American journalist of the area was killed by the police. His death brought an outcry from civil rights organizations across the nation and called attention to what one newspaper editor called "a justly aggrieved minority group."

After the Vietnam War, several occurrences deepened

CHICANOS ON THE MARCH. César Chávez became a nationally known Mexican-American leader in the 1960s, when he led the United Farm Workers in their drive to secure higher wages and better working conditions. The boycott of non-union produce set up by Chávez received wide support in many parts of the United States. *Wide World Photos*

public interest in Mexican Americans. The influx of illegal Mexican aliens discussed in earlier chapters concerned public officials and private citizens alike. But Americans who were alarmed by accounts of illegal immigration were also stirred by news from Mexico. According to newspaper reports, the Mexican government was concerned about the ill-treatment that some of its citizens received in the United States. In earlier years, that news might not have disturbed the average American. But in an oil-hungry world, an oil-rich nation such as Mexico had to be listened to with respect.

Perhaps the discovery of new, immensely productive oil fields in Mexico in the late 1970s did more than anything else to bring the Mexican Americans and their problems to the fore.

*　　*　　*

Enough has been said to indicate that the term "Mexican American" applies to a very large and a very diverse minority group—large because it numbers between seven and eight million citizens; diverse because it includes Americans residing in widely separated areas and living in highly different circumstances. In fact, according to Joan W. Moore, author of *The Mexican Americans,* Americans of Mexican descent are probably the most diverse of all immigrant minority groups in social composition. Members of the group include descendants of the Spaniards who came to New Mexico in the 16th century, as well as children born yesterday to undocumented parents who had just crossed the Rio Grande. Mexican Americans live in the isolated valleys of southern Colorado and in the heart of Los Angeles. Some Mexican Americans are Caucasian, some are Indian, and some are a mixture of the two races. The group includes highly educated people who speak elegant English, and others who are illiterate and can neither speak nor understand English. The Mexican-American minority includes governors, members of Congress, Roman Catholic bishops, diplomats, newspaper editors, and millionaire businessmen, along with poverty-stricken migrant workers.

The diversity of the Mexican-American population is revealed by the terminology used by members of the group

89

to describe themselves. "Latin" and its Spanish equivalent, "Latino," are the choice of some Mexican Americans, while others prefer to call themselves "Latin American" or "Spanish American." The Mexican Americans of New Mexico call themselves "Hispanos," to set them apart from the "Anglos," or English-speaking people. "Chicano," a name that is supposedly a simplification of "Mexicano," was first used by Mexican Americans who recognized the problems they faced in their efforts to obtain equality in American society.

In the beginning, "Chicano" had a militant connotation, and the word was popular with young Mexican Americans who were impressed by the Black Power movement. Chicano artists paid tribute to their Indian heritage in the murals they painted on buildings in the barrios, or Mexican-American neighborhoods, in major cities. Chicano literature and theater dealt with the Mexican Americans' struggle to win their "place in the sun." In recent years, "Chicano" has become almost synonymous with "Mexican American" in many parts of the country. Some militants now prefer to use "La Raza"—*raza* is the Spanish word for "race"—in referring to members of their minority group.

Diverse as the Mexican Americans are, they constitute a recognizable minority group because they have a number of common characteristics. While some Mexican Americans are proud of their European ancestry and others are equally proud of being Indian, the great majority have both Indian and European forebears. Spanish is the first or "home" language of most Mexican Americans. (The use of Spanish gives cohesion to the minority group, but creates social and economic problems that will be considered shortly.) Most

Mexican Americans are Roman Catholic, and the Church is a significant force in their communities. The strong family ties that characterize Mexican Americans are related to the influence of religion in their daily lives.

Mexican-American families are considerably larger than the average U.S. family. According to a 1981 Bureau of the Census report, "White Americans had 68.5 babies for every 1,000 women last year, as against 84.0 for black women and 106.6 among Hispanic women." The Mexican-American population is also younger than the national average, the Bureau of the Census reports. Twenty-six percent of the Mexican-American population of the United States is under 10 years of age, while the national average is 15 percent.

Mexican Americans are geographically concentrated. More than half of them live in California and Texas. New Mexico, Arizona, and Colorado are the home states of other large concentrations of Chicanos. Recent census returns show that many Mexican Americans are moving from other parts of the Southwest to California, and that smaller numbers are moving to the Pacific Northwest and the Midwest. Chicanos are not only concentrated in a few states—they are concentrated in certain sections of those states: southern Texas, northern New Mexico, southern California. Moreover, they are concentrated in the cities of those regions. Mexican Americans constitute about one-quarter of the population of Los Angeles and more than half the population of San Antonio.

*   *   *

The typical Mexican American is not a migrant worker, as some people suppose. Only 8.5 percent of employed Mexican-American men have agricultural jobs, and an even smaller percentage of Chicano women are farm workers. The great majority of employed Mexican-American men and women have blue-collar or white-collar jobs. In that respect, they resemble the American working population as a whole. But Mexican Americans are a disadvantaged economic group when compared with the working population of the United States in general. A 1981 census report gave their median family income as $15,200 a year, as compared with the national average of $19,661. Almost 20 percent of Mexican-American families live below the poverty line defined by the federal government. The national average of families living below the poverty line is approximately 9 percent.

Mexican Americans are an economically disadvantaged group for several reasons. As noted earlier, the typical Mexican-American family is larger than the average U.S. family. The number of children under 18 is higher than the norm, which means that Chicano families, on the average, have more dependent children than other American families. Since the typical Mexican-American family income is lower than the national average, parents must stretch fewer dollars to provide for a larger household. A lower living standard is the consequence.

Some economists and sociologists would consider the foregoing a surface explanation for economic disparities between Mexican Americans and the general population. Such experts are more interested in why Mexican Americans cannot get better-paying jobs that would raise the family income level.

Many Mexican Americans are disadvantaged from the moment they enter the job market because they are poorly educated. One in five adult Mexican Americans has had fewer than five years of schooling, and only one in three Chicanos over 25 years of age has completed high school, according to a recent study. There is a very high dropout rate among Mexican-American students, a fact that has concerned educators for many years.

It is not difficult to understand why Mexican-American children have had a far higher dropout rate than the school population as a whole. Chicano children were sent to separate and unequal schools in many Southwestern communities until Supreme Court decisions made the practice unconstitutional. The vast majority of the Chicano children in such schools knew no English when they entered, and their teachers knew no Spanish. Most teachers were not trained to teach English as a second language. Failing in their efforts to deal with Chicano pupils as they dealt with Anglo pupils, some frustrated teachers attempted to force Mexican-American children to learn English by punishing them for speaking Spanish. Other teachers came to regard their Mexican-American pupils as retarded and therefore incapable of learning.

Even after racially segregated public schools were declared unconstitutional, many local school boards evaded the Supreme Court ruling through token desegregation, or by authorizing a method of segregating children according to their "ability." Since the tests used in this system of classification were written in English, they discriminated against children whose "home" language was Spanish. As a result, Mexican-

American pupils were often classified as "slow learners." They were kept in the same grade for several years, or were assigned to classes for the retarded. In some public schools, Mexican-American children had little contact with their English-speaking peers, so they could not even pick up the basic English used on the playground. Discouraged because their needs were not met, Chicano children often dropped out of elementary school. Because they had not mastered English or acquired the basic skills needed in a highly competitive world, such children were handicapped for the rest of their lives.

The disadvantaged position of the Chicano child carried over into his or her youth. A long-term Department of Labor study released in 1980 indicated that "in almost every respect of their labor market experience, black and Hispanic youth are significantly worse off than white youth." The report cited the higher unemployment rate among minority youths, and the fact that they were laid off more frequently than their white counterparts. The report also pointed out that even when they were employed, young Hispanics and blacks were usually assigned to lower-paying, less skilled jobs than white youths.

A disadvantaged Mexican-American child almost inevitably becomes a disadvantaged youth, who it turn usually becomes a disadvantaged adult. When seeking employment, the typical Chicano man or woman has two obvious liabilities in the eyes of many employers: the applicant's skin is darker than that of most Anglos, and he or she speaks English inadequately. Although the applicant's ancestors may have lived in the United States for generations, the employer regards him or her as a foreigner. And when the applicant's limited schooling is noted, the employer is likely to offer nothing better than a low-paying job that requires little skill.

Job discrimination is not limited to employers. Some labor unions exclude Mexican Americans, despite union rules and federal law, or discriminate against them in the hiring hall. In *The Chicano Worker,* Vernon M. Briggs and his coauthors report that the Longshoremen's Association (AFL-CIO) in Houston, one of the nation's largest ports, has three separate unions—one for Anglos, one for blacks, and one for Mexican Americans. The unions for minority members are assigned the loading of dirty and dangerous cargoes.

Discrimination against Mexican Americans in schools and places of employment is closely related to discrimination against them in housing. Almost every town and city in the Southwest has its Chicano section, known to its residents as *el barrio* ("the neighborhood") and referred to in the Anglo part of town as Little Mexico. The word "ghetto" has a harsh sound, but it accurately describes the deteriorated section of town where Mexican Americans tend to be concentrated. Chicanos may be localized in a few shacks on the edge of a desert village, or in a large section of a metropolis. A good example is East Los Angeles, the most populous Mexican-American community in the United States. The barrio sprawls among factories, warehouses, and freeways. While it is part of a great metropolis, East Los Angeles is isolated by its poverty.

When tourists visit a Chicano barrio, they may be charmed by what they see and hear. The neighborhood seems colorful and bursting with life. The casual visitor does not sense the feelings of hopelessness and desperation that afflict many people living in "the neighborhood." But social workers and others who know the barrio understand why violence sometimes erupts. Youth, unable to find any kind of legitimate work, may engage in gang warfare to relieve their boredom. Jobless parents may deal in drugs to support their children, or resort to crime in order to acquire the financial status that Anglo society seemingly denies them.

Chicano leaders point out that there is no more violence in a barrio than in an Anglo ghetto of similar size. But Chicano leaders believe that their neighborhoods are subject to more harassment by law-enforcement officers. Until such raids were prohibited by a court order, agents of the Immigration and Naturalization Service periodically swept through East Los Angeles and other barrios, entering homes, business establishments, and public places, and questioning Spanish-speaking people. During these raids, both American citizens and illegal aliens were intimidated by federal agents.

Newspaper reports indicate that Mexican Americans are still victims of brutality at the hands of state and local law-enforcement officers. A recent case that attracted nationwide attention involved three Houston policemen who arrested a young Chicano during a barroom disturbance. The officers beat the young man severely and threw him into a creek because one of the policemen wanted "to see if a wetback can swim." (Far from being an alien, the young Chicano was a native of Houston who had served in the Vietnam War.) Two days later, the body of the young man was found in the creek. The officers who had arrested him were immediately dismissed from the Houston police force. Having been charged with homicide, they were tried in a state criminal court. When the jury found the accused officers innocent, Chicano leaders and representatives of civil rights organizations expressed outrage.

The U.S. Department of Justice then had the three policemen brought to trial for violating federal civil rights laws by causing the death of the Chicano youth. The trial in federal district court resulted in a guilty verdict, but the judge placed the convicted parties on probation instead of imposing prison sentences. The Department of Justice appealed the sentence to a higher court on the grounds that probation was not a permissible sentence in cases where the possible penalty was life imprisonment. The U.S. Court of Appeals ordered the federal district judge to impose prison terms on the three policemen. The judge did as he was ordered: he imposed prison terms of a year and a day. The national president of the League of United Latin American Citizens called the sentences a disgraceful misuse of federal power and demanded the impeachment of the judge who had imposed minimum sentences for a shocking crime.

Officers of the Mexican-American Legal Defense and Educational Fund pointed out that the murder of the young man in Houston was not an isolated case. They cited many other examples to support their charges that Mexican Americans in Southwestern communities were frequent victims of police brutality. Chicano leaders declared that even when officers were brought to trial for mistreating Mexican Americans, all-Anglo juries were likely to acquit the accused parties, and that in cases where accused officers were found guilty, Anglo judges were likely to impose minimum sentences. Accusations of police brutality made by Chicano leaders were recognized by a recent regulation of the U.S. Department of Justice. The department warned municipal police officials that they risked losing federal funds if they engaged in brutal treatment of members of minority groups.

When Americans of Mexican descent are discriminated against, or are victims of police brutality in the United States, the incidents are widely reported in the major newspapers of Mexico. Such publicity creates animosity toward the United States, and adversely affects diplomatic relations between the two republics.

*　　*　　*

Police brutality in the 1960s and 1970s provided an incentive for Chicano leaders to bring their fellow Mexican Americans into organizations such as those cited in connection with the Houston case. Economic disadvantage was another reason for promoting cooperative effort in Chicano neighborhoods; dissatisfaction with educational status was yet another motivating force. Mexican-American leaders who regarded their lack of political "clout" as the basis of Chicano difficulties in the 1950s began a campaign to increase their power at all levels of government. Later on, young Mexican Americans who were affected by the unrest that swept high schools and colleges during the Vietnam War set up organizations aimed at improving the educational and economic status of their age group.

In some communities, federal agencies such as the Office of Economic Opportunity have encouraged Mexican Americans to set up organizations that would develop leadership and encourage participation in the socioeconomic management of the communities. In other cases, Chicano organizations have developed self-help programs on their own. For example, the East Los Angeles Community Union recently raised the funds to build a $32 million industrial park that will employ 2,000 workers in its various factories. In the words of the director of the Community Union, "We want to get people off welfare and build a healthy economic community."

Chicano youth organizations have taken many forms. Some were support groups for the striking farm workers led by César Chávez. Other youth organizations have focused attention on education by demanding provisions for Chicano studies in high schools and colleges, the employment of more bilingual teachers, and increased minority admissions to colleges and universities.

Chicanos have aroused the most interest, and perhaps the most antagonism among Anglo-Americans, through political activity. Events in Crystal City, Texas, provide a striking example. This seat of government in a county largely populated by Mexican Americans had always been under the control of a small group of Anglo ranchers and merchants. In 1966, several Chicano citizens decided that the time had come to put members of the majority group on the school board and town council. A political party, La Raza Unida ("The United Race"), was organized, and it conducted a voter registration drive so that all eligible Chicanos would be qualified to vote. At the same time, the leaders of the new party preached Chicano unity as the means of winning elections.

The new political party gained control of the school board

and town council, as planned. But the Chicano leaders lacked educational background, knowledge of government, and political experience. It was several years before they learned how to run a school system and a town government. In the meantime, they antagonized a large part of the Anglo community by making the needs of the Chicanos the first priority. In fact, one of the first moves of the Crystal City Chicanos was to make drastic changes in the school system. With the aid of funds and advice supplied by the U.S. Office

CHICANO POLITICAL CLOUT. When the political party organized by the Mexican-American majority in Crystal City, Texas, took control of the municipal government in 1966, the impact was felt throughout the Southwest. Chicano activists also set up social and economic organizations that implemented their political influence. *Wide World Photos*

of Education, a system of bilingual and bicultural education was introduced. Its object was to make all students, Anglo and Chicano alike, fluent in two languages and appreciative of two cultures.

Chicano success in Crystal City influenced political events in other parts of the Southwest. Under the direction of the Southwest Voter Registration project, Chicanos were instructed in the use of the ballot as a means of improving their status in American society. As the presidential election of 1976 approached, 488,000 Texas Chicanos registered to vote. The Mexican-American vote, by tradition heavily Democratic, was credited with Jimmy Carter's narrow margin of victory in a crucial state. As the 1980 election neared, 800,000 Chicanos were registered, and both the Republican and the Democratic presidential candidates courted the Mexican Americans of Texas.

In their quest for political influence, Mexican Americans have had the support of the U.S. Department of Justice, which enforces the Voting Rights Act. Thus, in 1979, the department barred Houston and Dallas, the largest cities in Texas, from holding municipal elections until they had devised a system of government that would adequately represent ethnic minorities. In 1980, both Houston and Dallas adopted systems that assured the election of members of minority groups to the city councils. Political scientists predicted that, having secured representation in this manner, Mexican Americans would play a larger role in Texas politics.

Evidence of the growing political influence of Mexican Americans has made some Anglo-Americans uneasy. The feeling is particularly marked in Texas, where the memory of its war of independence is kept alive, and where the Chicano "takeover" of Crystal City created misgivings about the future. The Mexican Americans' insistence on speaking Spanish and preserving their culture concerns people who regard assimilation as the proper goal of all minority groups. Anglo-Americans familiar with the works of Chicano writers sometimes profess to be alarmed when they read about "Aztlán," the ill-defined geographical and political entity that some militant Mexican Americans say they want to create in the Southwest. The very mention of this vague sort of Chicano separatism makes nervous Anglo-Americans think of Canada, where French separatism threatens the stability of the nation.

Such fears reflect the latent hostility that exists between some Mexican Americans and their Anglo counterparts. This antagonism is rooted in the closely intertwined histories of Mexico and the United States, which will be reviewed in the next three chapters.

6

Past Conflicts, Present Disputes

A sentry had been posted in the belfry of the village church to raise an alarm when the attacking army came in sight. From that vantage point he could look toward the distant Rio Grande, which General Santa Anna was reported to have crossed several days before on his march to San Antonio. Below the belfry, the sentry could see his fellow Texans strengthening their fortress, commonly known as the Alamo, after the Spanish word for the cottonwoods that grew nearby. The Alamo had once been a thriving Franciscan mission, but now it was something of a ruin. Yet even though the roofs of its various buildings had collapsed, the surrounding wall was of thick masonry, and it was high. Debris and earth had been mounded at strategic points along the wall, and on these emplacements 20 cannons had been mounted. Food had been stored, and ammunition collected, in preparation for a siege.

The sentry shivered, perhaps from the cold, perhaps from the sight of the Mexican army, its lances flashing in the rising sun, its pennants aflutter in the breeze. The sentry grabbed the rope, tolled the bell, and joined his fellow Texans inside the Alamo. A fateful battle in the joint history of Mexico and the United States was about to begin.

Inside the Alamo were men who were already famous, including Davy Crockett and Jim Bowie (inventor of the knife that bore his name), and men who were to become famous because of their exploits in the next 12 days. Among the latter was William B. Travis, who commanded the defenders. Supporting him were approximately 175 Texans who had chosen to withstand a siege. Travis was depending upon the famed marksmanship of his riflemen to hold off however many soldiers were in Santa Anna's army. He called his men Texans, but the description was not entirely accurate—there were a number of Mexicans in his force, and several Europeans. Most of the defenders, however, were American-born.

The Texans had not yet declared their independence although they had been at war with Mexico for more than a year. The men inside the Alamo were fighting Santa Anna because he had made himself a dictator, having set aside the Mexican constitution, which was modeled on the Constitution of the United States. The issue was whether the freedoms to which Americans were accustomed would be respected in Texas, the Mexican province where the defenders of the Alamo had settled.

The Mexican force made a brave show as it neared San Antonio. The officers had excellent mounts, and their uniforms were colorful. A band played marching tunes; the cavalry raised a wall of dust; tramping soldiers and rumbling field guns shook the ground. But the formidable appearance of the army belied its true condition. Many of the foot soldiers were Indians who had been forced into the army. They were unfamiliar with the Spanish language and unaccustomed to military discipline. And Santa Anna's men, infantry and cavalry alike, were tired and hungry after their forced march.

Antonio López de Santa Anna, president of the Republic of Mexico and commander-in-chief of its armed forces, had led his troops to San Antonio to crush a rebellion mounted by Americans—those arrogant colonists who had long defied Mexican authority and now were making war against their own government. Since Santa Anna was, in effect, the Mexican government, the Texans had challenged his very person. To crush the uprising, Santa Anna had brought a force of impressive size. But, conscious of the inner weakness of his outwardly imposing army, and respectful of the defenders' warlike reputation, Santa Anna made a peaceful overture. In his own words, he "offered life to the defendants who would surrender their arms and retire under oath not to take them up again against Mexico." The defenders rejected Santa Anna's offer out of hand.

The Mexican general ordered that a red flag be flown

from the belfry of the village church, which he had occupied. That was the signal for a battle in which no prisoners would be taken.

*   *   *

The siege of the Alamo began on February 24, 1836. At first, the advantage lay with the defenders. The walls of the Alamo were too thick for the field guns of the Mexicans to batter down, while the cannons of the Texans prevented assault parties from approaching the fortress walls. Meanwhile, the withering fire of the defending riflemen took hundreds of Mexican lives.

Santa Anna finally decided to storm the Alamo. Before daylight on March 6, he divided his army into four brigades and provided each with axes, iron bars, and ladders for scaling the walls. At dawn, a bugler signaled the assault; the band struck up a war song that warned of throat-cutting. The gruesome sound aroused the defenders to a frenzy. A line of marksmen atop the walls mowed down the approaching soldiers as if they were blades of grass, but there were always more troops to replace the ones that fell. Although the attacking columns were forced back again and again, they kept returning, each time drawing closer to the walls. At length, a Mexican column breached the south wall and poured into the fortress.

The battle moved from the walls to the buildings. Overpowered by waves of Mexican soldiers, the defenders fell in crumpled heaps. In its final stage, the battle raged in the chapel, the last stronghold of the Texans. There the hand-to-hand struggle ended with the death of all the remaining defenders.

The Mexican victory at the Alamo was followed by another—one of Santa Anna's generals defeated a Texan force of 300 near the town of Victoria. The prisoners surrendered with the understanding that they would be disarmed and then paroled. But when Santa Anna was informed of the surrender, he gave orders that the prisoners be shot. Accordingly, the Texans were marched to Goliad and executed outside that town.

The fall of the Alamo and the mass execution at Goliad aroused all Texans. During the siege of the Alamo, they had declared their independence—henceforth Texas was to be a sovereign nation and not part of Mexico. Sam Houston, the Texan commander-in-chief, called for recruits and got them by the hundreds. Since his force was still much smaller than the one Santa Anna commanded, Houston enticed his enemy to follow him eastward, thus extending the Mexican supply line to the danger point. When Houston was satisfied that the Mexican force was sufficiently weakened by his tactic, he surprised Santa Anna at San Jacinto, near the present city that bears the Texas hero's name. The Texans fell on the Mexican army with a battle cry that became famous: "Remember the Alamo! Remember Goliad!" The Mexican forces were routed, and Santa Anna was captured. As the price of his release, the Mexican ruler was forced to acknowledge that Texas had gained its independence.

*   *   *

In fighting Santa Anna's armies during their war for independence, Texans of American descent developed an enmity for Mexicans, despite the fact that Texans of Mexican ancestry were among the defenders of the Alamo, and that patriots of Mexican descent were also among the signers of the Texas declaration of independence. The image of Mexico created during the Texas Revolution was perpetuated by the Anglo-American authors of the history books that were studied by generations of Texan schoolchildren. Reading such histories fixed the idea of their superiority in the minds of pupils of Anglo descent. On the other hand, reading about Santa Anna put many young Texans of Mexican ancestry on the defensive. In *Foreigners in Their Native Land,* David J. Weber says, "The events of March 6, 1836, at the Alamo have contributed more to Mexican-American schoolchildren's loss of self-esteem than any other historical episode. Children learn that thousands of Mexicans needlessly and wantonly slaughtered some 175 Americans who courageously chose to die."

Most Anglo schoolchildren never read about the Mexican case against their forebears. The hostility that developed between Mexicans and Texans had explanations besides the conduct of Santa Anna. In 1821, when the Mexican government authorized Moses Austin to settle 300 American families in the province of Texas, it was with the understanding that in return for extremely generous grants of land, the settlers would accept certain conditions. They were to take an oath of allegiance to Mexico, signifying that they accepted its sovereignty. Since slavery had been abolished throughout Mexico, Americans were not to bring their slaves to Texas. And since Mexico was officially Roman Catholic in religion, the settlers would have to accept that faith.

Most of the Americans who settled in the Mexican province of Texas ignored the rules made by the Mexican government. Many failed to take the oath of allegiance, and of those who did, most continued to regard themselves as Americans. Many settlers brought their slaves, and most remained staunchly Protestant.

As settlers poured into Texas from the United States, Mexican officials became alarmed at the prospect of an American takeover of their province, and the frontier between Texas and the United States was officially closed in 1830. Nevertheless, Americans continued to enter illegally in great numbers, because the long, ill-defined boundary could not be sealed by the forces that Mexico had at its command. In 1831, the estimated American population of Texas was 20,000; five years later the number had increased to 52,000.

The ethnic distribution of the population of Texas on the eve of revolution helps to explain why Santa Anna mounted his campaign. In 1836, the population of Texas was approximately 7 percent Mexican, 10 percent black, 28 percent Indian, and 55 percent Anglo-American, according to Texas historian Joe B. Franz. To prevent Americans from overthrowing Mexican authority in Texas, Santa Anna resolved to act.

Santa Anna's campaign not only led to the establishment of the Republic of Texas—it also heightened American interest in Mexican territory lying between the western boundary of the United States and the Pacific Ocean. Accounts of Santa Anna's perfidy at the Alamo and at Goliad were widely read in the United States. They created animosity toward Mexico and a feeling of kinship with the Texans. But American interest in Texas predated the events of 1836 by many years. The Louisiana Purchase had given the United States a poorly defined boundary with Spanish America. When Mexico gained its independence in 1821, it succeeded Spain as a neighbor of the United States. And after thousands of Americans settled in Texas, the United States assumed a vested interest in that part of Mexico.

To pro-slavery leaders in the United States, Texas was a territory that might be admitted to the Union as one or more slave states to balance the free states that were being created in the North. Meanwhile, the thriving trade that had developed between cities along the Mississippi and far-away Santa Fe forged close ties between New Mexico and the United States. Americans engaged in the Santa Fe trade increasingly thought of New Mexico as a future part of their own country.

Enterprising American capitalists sometimes looked even farther afield than New Mexico. The splendid harbors and the natural resources of California invited the kind of development that Americans liked to undertake. The fact that California reputedly was coveted by Great Britain made its acquisition doubly necessary, in the opinion of some Americans. It was the age of imperialism—European powers were staking their claims to far-flung colonies. If the United States did not thwart Britain and France, one or the other of those great powers might annex California and also bring the newly established Republic of Texas under its domination.

In the United States, the urge was to expand into adjoining territories, rather than to acquire distant colonies. "Manifest Destiny" was the name given to that urge. In a mystical

110

sense, the words implied that God intended for the people of the United States to occupy the North American continent from ocean to ocean. In a practical sense, Manifest Destiny was the justification for thwarting Great Britain in its designs on Oregon, and for depriving Mexico of a large part of its territory. In an effort to expand westward, the United States had attempted to purchase Texas prior to its war of independence. That effort failed, but after Texas declared its independence, the new nation asked to be annexed to the United States. At first, the request was denied—more for reasons of domestic politics than out of fear of the Mexican government's warning that the annexation of Texas would be considered an act of war.

The acquisition of Texas became a principal campaign issue in the presidential election of 1844. James K. Polk, the Democratic candidate, a declared advocate of annexation, led what was referred to by his opponents as "the war party." Henry Clay, the Whig candidate, was regarded as the peace advocate. Polk's victory led to an outbreak of "Texas fever"—a warlike mood that gripped the nation. However, it was not Polk who had Texas admitted to the Union. In one of the last acts of his administration, President John Tyler, Polk's predecessor, urged Congress to admit Texas to the Union by joint resolution. When Congress complied, the United States took a major step toward war with Mexico.

*   *   *

The dislike that Americans developed for Mexicans during the Texas Revolution was more than matched by the

111

fear and distrust of Americans that Mexicans developed as a result of their war with the United States in 1846–1848. That conflict, referred to in history books published in the United States as the Mexican War, is sometimes referred to as the American Invasion in textbooks published in Mexico. The conduct and the outcome of that war poisoned relations between Mexico and the United States for generations.

For one thing, the war of 1846–1848 brought into relief some basic attitudes that Americans displayed toward Spaniards and Indians, the forebears of the Mexican people. As the descendants of Britons who fought the Spaniards for world domination in the era of Queen Elizabeth I, many Americans accepted the "black legend" as truth. According to that view of history, the cruel, warlike Spaniards were guilty of endless villainy until their power was curbed by British might. Americans of Dutch descent remembered accounts of the Spanish persecution of their Protestant ancestors in the Netherlands, and added religious bigotry to the list of sins attributed to Spaniards. And since the British and the Dutch developed democratic institutions, while Spain adhered to absolute monarchy, the northern European nations had further reason to feel superior to their Spanish rival.

The British who settled in what is now the United States had a very different attitude toward race than that displayed by the Spaniards who settled in what is now Mexico. The Spaniards did not regard the white race as superior to all others. On the contrary, they rejected the idea of racial discrimination and freely intermarried with the Indians whom they conquered.

VOLUNTEERS !

Men of the Granite State!
Men of Old Rockingham !! the
strawberry-bed of patriotism, renowned for bravery and devotion to Country, rally at this call. Santa Anna, reeking with the generous confidence and magnanimity of your countrymen, is in arms, eager to plunge his traitor-dagger in their bosoms. To arms, then, and rush to the standard of the fearless and gallant **CUSHING**---put to the blush the dastardly meanness and rank toryism of Massachusetts. Let the half civilized Mexicans hear the crack of the unerring New Hampshire rifleman, and illustrate on the plains of San Luis Potosi, the fierce, determined, and undaunted bravery that has always characterized her sons.

Col. **THEODORE F. ROWE**, at No. 31 Daniel-street, is authorized and will enlist men this week for the Massachusetts Regiment of Volunteers. The compensation is **$10 per month---$30 in advance**. Congress will grant a handsome bounty in money and **ONE HUNDRED AND SIXTY ACRES OF LAND**.

Portsmouth, Feb. 2, 1847.

WAR FEVER. Stirred by broadsides, such as this example, thousands of young men volunteered to serve in the war against Mexico—a war denounced as unjust by a number of prominent Americans. *The Library of Congress*

Anglo-Saxons who settled along the Atlantic seaboard began the extermination of the native Indians, whom they considered inferior because they were a darker race than

Europeans. The association of inferiority with dark skin persisted among Americans even after they drew up the Declaration of Independence, with its bold assertion of equality.

The hostility that great numbers of Americans had developed toward Indians and Spaniards was displayed when the annexation of Texas brought war with Mexico. The prospect of fighting a Catholic people of mixed Spanish-Indian blood appealed to those Americans who believed that they were superior because they were white Anglo-Saxon Protestants.

The annexation of Texas in 1845 made war inevitable in Mexican eyes, but President Polk tried diplomacy before he resorted to force. He sent John Slidell to the Mexican capital to secure satisfaction for damages that American citizens had suffered to their property during the periodic civil wars that had devastated Mexico since it gained its independence from Spain in 1821. Slidell also was instructed to negotiate the purchase of New Mexico and California.

When the Mexican government refused to sell the territory that President Polk wanted to add to the United States, he decided to take by force of arms what he could not secure by diplomacy. Polk ordered General Zachary Taylor to move his troops from Louisiana into Texas and to occupy the territory between the Nueces and the Rio Grande. When Taylor advanced into an area that Mexicans regarded as part of their nation, they attacked. As soon as President Polk learned of the battle, he went before Congress and charged that "American blood has been shed on American soil." At the president's urging, Congress declared war on May 13, 1846.

The war appeared to be popular with the general public, but strong opposition was voiced in some quarters. Among the opponents of war was Abraham Lincoln, then a member of the House of Representatives from Illinois. Lincoln challenged President Polk to prove that Mexico had begun hostilities, as claimed. The young congressman accused the president of marching an army out of the United States into an area not proved to be American territory, thereby causing the first bloodshed of the war.

Alexander Stephens, a congressman from Georgia and later vice-president of the Confederacy, was bitter in his condemnation of the war, saying, "No man can tell for what object it is prosecuted. And it is to be doubted whether any man, save the President and his Cabinet, knows the real and secret designs that provoked its existence." Various other members of Congress, and such literary figures as Henry David Thoreau and James Russell Lowell also denounced the war.

Some European military experts believed that Mexico would repel an American invasion. A French general claimed that for all their cockiness, Americans were incapable of waging a successful war. *The London Times,* in surveying the developing war between Mexico and the United States, referred to the "disgraceful" behavior of American volunteers in the War of 1812 as indicative of the fact that "the Yankees will most certainly meet their Waterloo."

But more knowledgeable military experts believed that the United States was the advantaged nation in its war with Mexico. At the time, the two nations were roughly comparable in area, but the population of the United States, approximately 21 million, was about three times that of Mexico.

Moreover, a large part of the Mexican population consisted of impoverished Indians. In manpower, the United States had a clear advantage.

Mexico also was vulnerable because its population was concentrated in the highlands, with the national capital at the center. Most of Mexico was thinly garrisoned, and the area adjacent to the United States was virtually defenseless. As a rising industrial power, the United States could produce war materiel on a large scale and transport it to the battleground. In contrast, Mexican industry was poorly developed, and the transportation system was primitive.

But the major disadvantage that Mexico suffered as it faced the enemy was the chaotic state of its government. Santa Anna and his rivals had made the presidency of Mexico a political merry-go-round: one general would seize power and make himself dictator, only to be toppled in short order. Even though the Mexican people rallied to defend their country from the invading Americans, their efforts were often misdirected by leaders who were both inept and corrupt.

Five military expeditions moved against Mexico during the war of 1846–1848. The Army of the West, commanded by Colonel Stephen Kearny, set out for New Mexico on the Santa Fe Trail a few weeks after Congress declared war. The resistance that Kearny expected as he approached Santa Fe crumbled, and the Army of the West occupied the town without firing a shot. Kearny then dispatched Colonel Alexander Doniphan to complete the conquest of New Mexico, move south and occupy the northern part of Mexico. After defeating the Mexican force that opposed him, Doniphan continued his march southward and joined his

THE FINAL CAMPAIGN. General Scott's seizure of the key port of Veracruz in 1847 paved the way for the American occupation of the Mexican capital, thus ending the war.

The Library of Congress

forces with those of General Zachary Taylor.

Having taken Santa Fe, Kearny pressed on to California, where the third campaign against Mexico was developing. American settlers in northern California overthrew the Mexican authorities and declared the independence of what had been a Mexican province. Colonel John Frémont, an American officer in California presumably on a geographical survey, hurried to Sonoma to assist the rebels. In the meantime, Commodore John Sloat, who commanded an American flotilla that patrolled the California coast, occupied the port of Monterey. Sloat then proclaimed that all of California was part of the United States.

Mexican forces in southern California defeated the Americans who had seized Los Angeles and San Diego. Only the timely arrival of Stephen Kearny and his seasoned troops, after a forced march from New Mexico, prevented the reestablishment of Mexican authority in southern California. With the defeat of the Mexican militia at San Gabriel in January, 1847, the war in California came to an end.

By that time, General Taylor had overcome Mexican forces stationed along the Rio Grande and had penetrated far into Mexico. In September, 1846, he took the fortified city of Monterrey in a five-day battle. Taylor's most notable victory came in February, 1847, when he defeated Santa Anna in one of the most decisive engagements of the war. Taylor's victory was considered remarkable because his force had been weakened by the diversion of many of his troops to General Winfield Scott's army, which was preparing to make an amphibious landing at Veracruz.

The final campaign of the war began when Scott put 12,000 troops ashore and, after a three-day bombardment, succeeded in reducing the fortress that guarded Veracruz, the chief port of Mexico. Having occupied the city, Scott led his army toward the Mexican capital along the route that Cortez used when he scaled the mountains between the Gulf of Mexico and the tableland located a mile and a half above sea level.

The Mexican forces contested Scott's army all the way, taking a heavy toll in American lives. Even after troops commanded by Santa Anna were forced from the mountain stronghold of Cerro Gordo, the Mexican army's resistance did not lessen. In fact, as the Americans approached their capital city, Mexican soldiers and civilians alike showed an increasing determination to prevent the enemy from occupying their capital. Tribute to the defenders was paid by General Ulysses S. Grant in his memoirs. As a young lieutenant, Grant fought in the war of 1846–1848. Looking back to those years, he said of the Mexicans who fought against him: "I have seen as brave stands made by some of these men as I have ever seen made by soldiers."

After reducing the fortresses on the outskirts of Mexico City, the Americans stormed the final stronghold—Chapultepec, a castle long considered impregnable because it was protected by steep cliffs. A few days later—on September 14, 1847—General Scott led his army in triumph to the immense square that is the heart of Mexico City.

The Mexican people, who felt that they had been defeated as much by the misrule of their leaders as by the military prowess of the enemy, suffered the humiliation of seeing the capital of their nation occupied by a foreign army. The Mexicans had not only suffered a disastrous defeat—many individuals suffered physically at the hands of the invaders. After the war ended, several leaders of the victorious armies described injustices inflicted on the Mexican people by American soldiers. The volunteers who composed the greater part of the American army frequently pillaged towns and shot civilians. Such misdeeds led Captain E. Kirby Smith to write that "their conduct toward the poor inhabitants has been horrible, and their coming is dreaded like death in every village in Mexico." General Winfield Scott used stronger language in describing the crimes of robbery, rape, and murder committed by his troops when they got out of hand. The soldiers "committed atrocities to make Heaven weep and every American of Christian morals blush for his country."

But personal injury and the humiliation of defeat were less painful for patriotic Mexicans than the terms imposed by the Americans in the treaty that ended the war. The government of the United States agreed to settle the claims that American citizens had laid against Mexico for damages to their property before the war, and to pay $15 million for the territory it took. Mexicans regarded the sum as paltry and something of an insult, considering the extent of the lands that the United States had taken by force of arms. Almost half of Mexico passed to American ownership through the Treaty of Guadalupe Hidalgo, which was signed on February 2, 1848.

*   *   *

In the same way that generations of American schoolchildren have had their views of Mexico colored by history books that describe the misdeeds of Santa Anna during the Texas Revolution, generations of Mexican schoolchildren have had their views of the United States colored by history books that describe the misdeeds of American soldiers and statesmen during the war of 1846–1848, and the terrible price they forced a weaker nation to pay for its defeat.

Military Phases of the War

WAR AND AFTERMATH OF WAR. In the decade 1845–1855, approximately half of the territory of Mexico became part of the United States. The transfer of the vast area created problems that are still unsolved.   *The Library of Congress*

7

Civil War:
American and Mexican

At about the time that Americans were tearing their country apart by fighting the Civil War, the Mexicans, too, were fighting among themselves. But in the 1860s Mexico was also invaded by a European army, and a foreign emperor was forced upon the Mexican people. The eyes of the world focused on Mexico during that period as a young Austrian archduke and his wife played out their tragic roles against a backdrop of civil war and foreign intervention. American historians have paid much attention to this episode, because the United States played a part in preventing the downfall of the Republic of Mexico and the establishment of a monarchy.

Actually, the events that brought Maximilian and Carlota

to the Mexican throne began to unfold some years before the royal pair were persuaded to accept the crown. Even Santa Anna, the off-again-on-again president of Mexico, played a minor role in the drama. Despite the fact that he had led his country into a disastrous war with the United States, Santa Anna retained control of the Mexican government for a time. Having squandered what money he could raise at the end of the war of 1846–1848, Santa Anna was in need of funds to keep himself in power. In 1853, to secure the money he required, he sold part of his country to the United States for $10 million. The land involved in the Gadsden Purchase (so named for the American who bargained with Santa Anna) became the southern part of Arizona and New Mexico. Eventually, a transcontinental railroad was built across it.

A number of Mexicans were outraged by Santa Anna's sale of the Gadsden Purchase territory. Among them was Benito Juárez, a Zapotec Indian who was to become one of the most honored of all Mexicans. When Juárez was a child, few Indians attended school, and many did not speak Spanish. But the boy was befriended by a wealthy man who paid for his education, and after that his rise was swift. Having finished school, Juárez became a lawyer and a political leader. As governor of his native state, Oaxaca, he attracted national attention by taking over a bankrupt government and managing it so honestly that when he left office *he* was still poor, but the state treasury had a surplus.

Because of his opposition to Santa Anna's dictatorship, Juárez was forced to spend some time in exile in the United States. He returned in time to participate in a revolt against the government, which by that time had fallen completely under the control of the army, the Church, and the great landowners. The Liberal Party, of which Juárez was a leader, challenged the Conservatives, who represented the privileged class. After an election placed the Liberals in power, Juárez was appointed minister of justice. In that position, he drafted a law that made the army and the Church subject to civil courts rather than to courts of their own establishment. A companion law provided for the forced sale of all Church properties not actually used for religious purposes.

The laws enacted by the Liberal government aroused the opposition of the Church, which then owned an estimated one-third of all the land in Mexico, as well as a large amount of gold and silver. Juárez and other leaders of the Liberal Party accused the Church of using its vast resources to block needed reform, and they passed laws prohibiting the clergy from interfering with the conduct of government. In a further effort to reduce Church influence in civil affairs, the Liberals deprived the clergy of their control over education, and set up a civil register of births, marriages, and deaths to replace Church jurisdiction over those vital records. The Reform Laws, designed to bring about the separation of church and state, were incorporated in the constitution of 1857, which was the legal basis of government in Mexico until it was supplanted by a similar but modernized constitution in 1917.

The adoption of the constitution of 1857 plunged Mexico into the worst civil war in its history. The great landowners, the army, and the Church all rose against the Indian leader who was taking away their privileges. Juárez, now president of Mexico, was supported by an army raised from the masses. He and his guerrillas were hounded from one part of Mexico to another.

In desperate need of money to maintain his embattled government, Juárez turned to the United States for assistance. President James Buchanan drove a hard bargain with the Mexican leader. In return for a loan of $4 million, Juárez agreed to grant the United States a perpetual right-of-way across the Isthmus of Tehuantepec, a short route between the Atlantic and Pacific oceans. In addition, the United States was given permission to build railroads across northern Mexico. President Juárez had to agree to let the United States protect those transit routes with its troops, and also to let the troops intervene, in an emergency, without the consent of Mexico. (Fortunately for the future relationship between Mexico and the United States, President Buchanan could not persuade the U.S. Senate to ratify the treaty he had negotiated.)

*　　*　　*

By 1861, Juárez had reached what some foreign observers regarded as the end of his career. The most powerful forces in Mexico were ranged against him. The archbishop of Mexico had gone to Rome and had secured the support of the Pope in bringing an end to what he considered "the persecution of the Church." Numbers of wealthy landowners had fled their country and were trying to persuade European rulers to intervene in Mexican affairs because, they said, their countrymen were incapable of governing themselves.

France, Spain, and Great Britain each had financial claims

against Mexico. For decades, Mexican governments had borrowed money abroad, always at high interest. Invariably, the loans benefited the lenders more than the borrower. By the time European bankers and politicians had taken their commission, and corrupt Mexican generals and politicians had lined their pockets, only a fraction of the borrowed money was left to go into the Mexican treasury. Since the full amount of the loan nevertheless had to be repaid, the government suffered a double penalty.

In 1861, with the Mexican treasury empty, Juárez announced a postponement of interest payments on foreign debts. European creditors were indignant when they learned that they would have to wait. And Juárez had financial worries other than the unpaid loans. Many foreigners whose Mexican holdings had been seized or damaged during the civil wars were bringing pressure on their home governments to force President Juárez to pay the reparations due them. Juárez recognized the legality of the claims, but was unable to pay them.

Finally, British, French, and Spanish officials held a meeting. At that conference, the three governments agreed to send a joint naval force to Mexico. The object was to take possession of major Mexican ports and collect customs duties, and to use the money to pay foreign claims.

It was not long before the British and Spanish governments discovered that the third party to the agreement had far more than the collection of a debt in mind. Napoleon III, nephew of the famous general, Napoleon I, had been elected president of the French Republic in 1848. Once he gained control of the government, he brought the republic to an end by declaring himself Emperor Napoleon III. He and his wife, Eugénie, were intent upon restoring to France the prestige that it had enjoyed during the first Napoleonic era. The collection of the Mexican debt gave Napoleon III the pretext that he needed to establish a French "presence" in the New World. The time was propitious, because civil war had broken out in the United States, making it impossible for the Americans to thwart his plans. Since Napoleon III had from the outbreak of hostilities been a partisan of the Confederacy, and since he fully expected it to win the civil war, he foresaw no opposition from America in the years ahead.

The emperor could send as many troops to Mexico as were needed to establish French control. All he required now was some European prince to put at the head of the puppet government that he proposed to set up. Empress Eugénie was familiar with the courts of Europe, and had friends among the wealthy Mexican refugees then living in Paris. She suggested a likely candidate: Archduke Maximilian, a brother of the Emperor of Austria. He was personable, intelligent, and well-connected. Since he was popular with the Austrian people, he should appeal to the Mexicans, who were said to be warmhearted. His wife was beautiful and ambitious. What better pair could Napoleon III have as emperor and empress of Mexico? They would be the perfect instrument of French policy in that unfortunate country.

It was easier to persuade the archduchess to accept the offer of the crown than to convince the archduke to undertake the mission that Napoleon III had in mind. Maximilian wanted to be sure that the Mexican people really desired him as their emperor. Moreover, he demanded French guarantees of military and financial aid—he wanted an army to put down the civil disorders for which Mexico was noted, and money enough to support a government until revenue could be raised within the country.

The Mexicans who wanted to drive Juárez from power conducted a vote among their supporters and informed Maximilian that the people of their country were overwhelmingly in favor of having him as their emperor. Napoleon III assured Maximilian that the large army that had already been sent to Mexico would be kept there as long as the new emperor needed it. That army, already 30,000 strong, was to be paid from the Mexican treasury.

*　　*　　*

Satisfied that his terms had been met, Maximilian accepted the crown of Mexico. The new emperor and empress sailed for Mexico and reached Veracruz in May, 1864. Their reception upon arrival was the first of many shocks they were to suffer during their brief reign. They did not receive the tumultuous welcome that they had expected when their ship put into port—in fact, they regarded their reception as cold, if not actually hostile. But as the fatigued and disenchanted rulers neared Mexico City, their spirits lifted. Throngs of people lined the road, cheering their new sovereigns, and a delegation of aristocrats paid them homage.

But danger signals were already visible to anyone who dared to look. The troops that Napoleon III had sent to Mexico had driven Juárez and his guerrillas from the populous part of the country. "The Indian," as Juárez was derisively called by privileged Mexicans, had been forced to move his capital to the American border. But President Juárez did not admit that he had been defeated. French supply lines were often cut by his guerrillas, and wherever the invaders moved, they were harassed by the patriot army. Plainly, the majority of the Mexican people regarded Juárez as their champion.

The government of the United States had recognized Juárez as the rightful head of Mexico when he was elected president, and American public opinion supported him in his efforts to enforce the Reform Laws. But the outbreak of the American civil war made financial or military support to Juárez impossible.

The efforts of Napoleon III to persuade the British government to recognize the Confederacy aroused resentment in the United States, which was fighting to preserve the Union. Because of the war, the Lincoln administration could not invoke the Monroe Doctrine. However, the House of Representatives unanimously adopted a resolution declaring, "It does not accord with the policy of the United States to acknowledge any monarchical government erected on the ruins of any republican government in America under the auspices of any European power."

The resolution angered Napoleon III. But he had even more reason to be displeased with the Mexicans and with the rulers whom he had given them. Maximilian had declined to give Napoleon III the right to exploit the mineral wealth of the part of Mexico adjoining the United States. Moreover, despite the fact that Maximilian was a devout

Catholic, he had antagonized the Church by refusing to restore all its wealth and privileges. And even though his throne was supported by French bayonets, the Mexican emperor often questioned the tactics of Napoleon III's generals. Worst of all, the young emperor showed more sympathy for the Mexicans than for the French.

Maximilian and Carlota had been in Mexico little more than a year before Napoleon III abandoned his idea of creating a French empire in the New World. His intervention in Mexico had not brought his own people the glory that he had promised, nor the riches. Instead, the French were being asked to pay the cost of maintaining their soldiers in bankrupt Mexico and to bear the heavy casualties inflicted by Juárez' guerrillas.

Besides that, the Confederacy had not emerged victorious from the Civil War. The North had won, and already the United States was sending bold notes to Paris. To make matters worse, Americans were now smuggling arms across the Rio Grande for Juárez' army, while in New York, New Orleans, and other cities Americans were raising money for the Mexican president. And even more alarming news had reached Paris. The government of the United States had moved 25,000 soldiers commanded by General Philip Sheridan to a point that was within striking distance of the Mexican border. (Years later, Sheridan wrote in his autobiography that Juárez would never have been victorious without the help of the United States.)

*   *   *

The Empress Carlota's correspondence with the Empress

Eugénie paints a vivid picture of Mexico in the final stages of the French intervention. "Life here seems quite like the Middle Ages," she wrote. "One moment we are gay, comfortable, and serene, only to realize that at any moment a band of guerrillas may fall upon us." Napoleon III's decision to abandon Mexico became known to Carlota through her friends in Europe. Her subsequent letters to Empress Eugénie were bitter and demanding. She reminded the French rulers of their promises.

But Napoleon III was in no position to fulfill his obligations. Another protest had arrived from the American government—the sharpest yet. The note, sent by Secretary of State Seward, referred to the armed forces that the President of the United States had "placed in a spot of observation." But the American statesman was not content with making this veiled threat; he went on to inquire just when the French emperor proposed to withdraw his troops from Mexico.

Not having secured promises of further support from Napoleon III and Eugénie by means of letters, Carlota resolved to go to France and plead her consort's case in person. Somewhat reluctantly, Maximilian allowed his wife to set out on a mission of dubious value. Dispatches from the French commander in Mexico made Maximilian's cause seem hopeless. As the French army of occupation moved from the interior toward the coast for embarkation, Juárez and his strengthening forces reoccupied the territory from which they had been driven.

Then depressing news reached Maximilian from Europe. The heartless reception that the French ruler had given the Mexican empress had unhinged Carlota's mind. Her

AN EMPEROR MEETS HIS DEATH. Maximilian, who stands on the right, gave the central place of honor to one of the Mexican generals who had remained loyal to him. *The Bettmann Archive, Inc.*

mental condition worsened when the Pope refused to intervene in Maximilian's behalf despite her tearful pleading. Made insane by grief and anger, Carlota was confined by her Austrian in-laws, and later by her own family in Belgium.

Maximilian spurned the opportunity to abdicate and return to Europe as the French army withdrew. The events that followed have often been compared with a Greek tragedy in which Fate determines the outcome. At the head of the Mexican force that remained faithful to him, and supported by Austrian and Hungarian troops who were loyal because he was their archduke, Maximilian took his stand in the city of Querétaro, some distance north of the capital. After defending Querétaro for more than two months, Maximilian and his generals were taken captive. The Emperor of Mexico was tried by a military court and condemned to death.

There was a worldwide reaction to the sentence. A leading American newspaper editor called upon President Juárez "not to stain with unnecessary cruelty the young republic, so gloriously reborn." European statesmen joined with diplomats stationed in Mexico in pleading for Maximilian's life. Princess Salm-Salm, an American married to a German nobleman who supported Maximilian, remained loyal to the emperor to the last. By refusing to be rebuffed, she succeeded in gaining an audience with Juárez. "I am grieved, *señora,*" the president said, "to see you on your knees before me; but if all the kings and queens of Europe were at your side, I could not spare his life. It is not I who takes it away; it is my people and the law, and if I do not do their will, the people would take his life and my own as well."

The emperor and his two Mexican generals were executed by a firing squad on June 19, 1867. Thus Maximilian died, and thus a heroic legend was born.

*　　*　　*

On September 15, 1910, the people of Mexico prepared to celebrate the 100th anniversary of their declaration of independence and the 80th birthday of the man who had been their ruler for a third of that century. Although the honored person was officially General José de la Cruz Porfirio Díaz, he was known to everyone as Don Porfirio, *don* being a title of respect among people who speak Spanish.

At midnight, Don Porfirio, tall and erect despite his many years, stepped onto the balcony of the National Palace. The enormous plaza in front of the palace was jammed with people who had come to pay homage to their country and its lifetime president. Don Porfirio marked the advent of Independence Day (September 16) by ringing the bell that Father Hidalgo had tolled in 1810 when he had proclaimed Mexico's independence from Spain. Then the president shouted the traditional cry: "Long live liberty! Long live independence! Long live the heroes! Long live the Mexican

HISTORIC SITE, HISTORIC EVENT. This drawing from *Harper's Weekly* (Oct. 12, 1867) shows Benito Juárez arriving at the National Palace—former headquarters of Cortez and the Spanish viceroys—as the triumphant president of Mexico.

The Library of Congress

people!" The response from the crowd below sounded like a roar in Don Porfirio's ears. Then the great cathedral bells began to ring, and fireworks lit the sky.

Dignitaries from all over the world had gathered in Mexico City for the week-long celebration of independence. But it was Don Porfirio whom they had really come to honor. This general who had been president for a generation had received so many medals and other decorations from foreign governments that there was not room enough for all of them on his resplendent uniform. Theodore Roosevelt had called him "the greatest statesman now living" and a leader who "has done for his country what no other living man has done for any country."

Among those invited to attend the celebration were a number of foreign journalists who had come to Mexico at the expense of the Díaz government. They not only wrote accounts of the brilliant events for their readers, but also reviewed the career of the Mexican president whose birthday was the occasion for such pageantry.

Porfirio Díaz began his ascent to power as an army officer fighting on the side of Benito Juárez. After distinguishing himself in the civil war caused by the adoption of the constitution of 1857, Díaz fought the French. In that war, he gained the reputation of being the most capable of the Mexican generals. Like many military officers, Díaz aspired to be president; he twice challenged Benito Juárez for that high office and was defeated. When Juárez died, he was succeeded by his vice-president, who filled out the term and then engineered his own election as president. Porfirio Díaz, having been thwarted again in his bid for the presidency, seized control of the government in 1876. He promised the war-weary Mexicans that he would conduct genuine elections thereafter, and that he would bring an end to revolution.

The self-appointed president ignored his first promise: there was no real election for the next 34 years. But Don Porfirio kept his second promise: there were no more revolutions. He put a stop to them in a manner that made him the model for Latin American dictators for many years to come.

*　　*　　*

Díaz began his career as the uncrowned ruler of Mexico with a display of political skill and caution. He made peace with the Church, which was allowed to resume control over education and to repossess the property it had lost during the Juárez era. As a general, Díaz understood the ambitions of the military. He provided the funds and the organizational skill to make the army into a pillar of his regime. He created another powerful military force that was even more beholden to him. During the long years of civil war and foreign intervention, Mexico had been plagued by bandits. Instead of suppressing the brigands, Díaz organized them into a new military force. He put his recruits into showy uniforms, and gave them the power to shoot on sight. He stationed his *"rurales"* in the countryside, where they became the darlings of merchants and landowners and the scourge of those who opposed Don Porfirio.

The acclaim that the Mexican president received from abroad derived mainly from the favors that he bestowed on foreign businessmen. The Díaz government deprived Indian villages of their communal lands by rejecting titles that rested on the memory of man from time immemorial, rather than on written deeds. Individuals or companies that surveyed "idle" lands received a large part of the acreage as their reward. One American company acquired about six million acres in this manner, while Mexican companies received even larger holdings.

Díaz surrounded himself with the now-famous *"científicos,"* principally lawyers and economists who were dedicated to science and progress. They were determined to modernize Mexico so that it could take its place among the advanced nations of the world. To implement their plans, Díaz invited American and European industrialists to exploit both the mineral wealth of Mexico and the country's large and docile work force.

The networks of telegraph and telephone lines, railroads, and highways that Díaz proudly showed on maps of Mexico gave his country the transportation and communications systems that a modern nation required. But the construction of the railroads, highways, and communications systems profited foreign bondholders and managers more than the Mexican people. And while thousands of Mexicans worked in the cotton mills and other factories built by American and European industrialists, the employees received low wages and the owners received high profits. Strikes were broken by the army, and bloodshed sometimes resulted.

One of the concessions that Don Porfirio gave to British and American oil companies was to have far-reaching effects in the years ahead. When Spain conquered what is now

Mexico, the Spanish monarchs retained control of subsoil rights. In other words, land grants to the conquering soldiers were for the surface only—whatever mineral wealth lay below the surface belonged to the Spanish monarchs. If he was given the right to exploit the subsoil, the holder of the grant paid the king a share of any minerals he found in recognition of royal ownership.

The Spanish system of subsoil ownership became part of Mexican law when the nation's ties with Spain were severed. Rights once belonging to the Spanish monarch passed to the Mexican government. But Porfirio Díaz revised the long-accepted system of subsoil ownership and, in effect, allowed foreign oil companies to operate on the Anglo-Saxon principle that possession of the surface brings with it the ownership of whatever lies underneath. Thus oil pumped from the ground enriched foreign companies, while the Mexican people received little benefit.

*   *   *

Most of the dignitaries who came to Mexico to help celebrate Don Porfirio's 80th birthday regarded him as a miracle worker. He had brought peace and stability to a nation that had been torn by civil war from the day it had become independent. He had led a backward country into the 20th century—he had given it railroads, telegraph lines, well equipped ports, and modern factories. He had so beautified Mexico City that it compared favorably with Paris, London, and Rome.

But astute observers knew that the Mexican people had paid dearly for Don Porfirio's projects. In ruling for the benefit of the few, Díaz had consigned the great majority to a life of misery. Urban Mexicans worked long days for a pittance. Rural Mexicans were reduced to peonage—they lived as landless peasants in bondage to the very people who had dispossessed them. The tranquility remarked upon by foreign visitors could not conceal the fact that Don Porfirio had established a repressive dictatorship. Members of the Mexican legislature and the supreme court were handpicked. The governors of the states were Díaz' appointees. Elections were rigged, and the constitution had been amended to allow Díaz to retain the presidency as long as he wanted it. Any Mexican who dared to criticize the government invited imprisonment; any Mexican who openly opposed the regime invited assassination.

"MAN ON HORSEBACK"—a term commonly used for a dictator—was appropriately applied to Porfirio Díaz, absolute ruler of Mexico, 1876–1911. *The Library of Congress*

Such thoughts were hard to dwell upon amidst the glitter of the long celebration of Don Porfirio's birthday. After watching bullfights, colorful parades, dance spectacles, and other entertainments on successive days, Don Porfirio's foreign guests came to the National Palace for the climax of the celebration. There they joined the diplomatic corps and the cream of Mexican society. The vast central courtyard of the palace had been converted into a ballroom where 150 musicians played, and 1,000 electric stars twinkled overhead. In the banquet hall, 500 servants in brilliant livery poured champagne and served delicacies from all parts of Mexico. At ten o'clock, Don Porfirio made his entrance with the wife of the Italian ambassador on his arm. As a signal honor, the American ambassador had been chosen to escort the president's young and beautiful wife.

The guests danced until dawn in an atmosphere that one journalist described as "a fairyland." None of the guests realized that, figuratively speaking, they were dancing on top of a volcano that was about to erupt.

8

American Involvement in the Mexican Revolution

He did not seem qualified to lead a revolution. In a country where a commanding presence was much admired, he was unimpressive: barely five feet, three inches tall, slight of build, and shrill of voice. In a country that swarmed with generals, he was the complete civilian. The vast majority of his countrymen lived in grinding poverty; his family was rich. Most Mexicans could not read or write; he had been educated in the United States and Europe. From every point of view, Francisco I. Madero should have been satisfied with things as they were, and shunned all thought of revolution. But it was Madero's fate to set cataclysmic forces in motion and to become a martyr of the revolution that he had unleashed.

By 1908, the year that Madero became a national hero, Porfirio Díaz had been president of Mexico for 32 years and was 78 years old. Now that Don Porfirio was in his dotage, his enemies sought change in various directions. Most of his opponents merely wanted to trade places with him; they never considered altering the system of exploitation that the old man had perfected. At the other extreme were a few radicals who believed that the salvation of their country lay in the destruction of its shameful political, social, and economic system.

Most of the radicals had been forced into exile by Don Porfirio's secret police. Foremost among the dissidents were the Flores Magón brothers, who fled to El Paso, to San Antonio, to Los Angeles, and then to St. Louis to elude Mexican agents. In their hiding places in the United States, the brothers printed newspapers that were smuggled across the border. The forbidden literature convinced a growing number of Mexicans that their country was due for a change—a drastic, shattering change. Madero was familiar with the ideas of the Flores Magón brothers, and he had even given them financial support. But he shrank from the prospect of a revolution that would destroy the old system and create a radically new social order. To his way of thinking, a few simple changes in the political system would set things aright. If the constitution of 1857 was respected, if presidents were confined to one term of office, and if the people were allowed to vote freely, then dictatorship would disappear, and with it the abuses of the Díaz era.

*   *   *

The dictator provided Madero with the opportunity to

disseminate his ideas. As yet another presidential election approached, Don Porfirio permitted an American journalist to interview him. The resulting article appeared in a magazine published in the United States. When it was translated and circulated by Mexican newspapers, the interview created a sensation. The dictator was reported to have said that Mexico was ready for a more democratic system of government, and that he planned to relinquish the presidency at the end of his current term.

The idea of a government headed by someone other than Don Porfirio seemed strange to most Mexicans. They were soon offered proposals for governmental changes by Francisco I. Madero. *The Presidential Succession in 1910* was the title of the thin volume that described how Mexico might move from dictatorship to democratic government. The author immediately became a rallying point for those opposed to "Porfirianism."

It soon became apparent that the old dictator had no intention of surrendering authority. In fact, he announced his candidacy for yet another presidential term. The lines were drawn. Inspired by the ideas put forward in Madero's book, the Anti-reelectionists held a national convention and nominated the author as their presidential candidate. In a campaign that took him to all parts of Mexico, Madero gained wide support.

Then Díaz struck at his opponent. First Madero was imprisoned, and then so were hundreds of his followers. The election was held according to schedule, and, to the surprise of no one, the Mexican congress declared that Porfirio Díaz had won yet another term of office.

Madero was released from prison, but was kept under

house arrest. Disguised as a workman, he escaped from Mexico late in 1910 and made his way to the United States. Once across the border, he declared the recent election null and void and proclaimed himself provisional president of Mexico. Madero's family had a number of important friends in the United States, and the rebellion against the Mexican dictatorship aroused considerable sympathy north of the Rio Grande—two factors that explained why the American government allowed the fugitive to wage his campaign against Díaz from Texas cities. But as fighting broke out just across the border, and as arms purchased from American dealers moved in greater quantity across the border, President Taft became uneasy—war in Mexico would threaten the security of the United States. Taft ordered the deployment of 20,000 American troops along the border. From that point on, the United States was directly involved in the Mexican Revolution.

Madero was now penniless, having spent his personal fortune in promoting revolution. Since he had worn out his welcome in the United States, he crossed into Mexico and took command of the rebel army that was gathering around Juárez, the city just across the border from El Paso, Texas. Although Madero knew nothing of military tactics, he showed considerable skill and great bravery in the ensuing battle with the Díaz army. He managed to hold his ill-disciplined troops together until they defeated the Juárez garrison. The defeat that the Díaz forces suffered at the border city was followed by the loss of several posts in the southern part of Mexico. In May, 1911, Don Porfirio finally realized that he had reached the end of his career.

The old man left Mexico with his family and much treasure, and lived out his days in Europe.

*   *   *

Madero's journey from Juárez to the Mexican capital was a triumph. The presidential train stopped at every town and village en route, to provide the people with an opportunity to overwhelm the victor with their gratitude. No Mexican had ever had so much expected of him as Francisco Madero, and no Mexican had ever faced more formidable obstacles. Both Mexican and American historians stress those obstacles when they appraise his brief career as president.

To the great landowners, the professional soldiers, the upper clergy, and the factory owners of Mexico, Madero was a dangerous man because he threatened their privileges. Foreign business interests regarded the new president with uneasiness, having grown accustomed to the favorable climate of the Díaz era. Americans had particular reason to be alarmed. In 1912, one of the U.S. consuls stationed in Mexico estimated that American investments in Mexican oil lands and refineries, mines and smelters, agricultural lands, railroads, and other properties totaled more than $1 billion, which was a large part of the total wealth of Mexico.

Madero met with opposition among the privileged. At the same time, he angered those who spoke for the dispossessed. Foremost among the latter was Emiliano Zapata, a guerrilla leader whose battle cry, "Land and Liberty!" had rallied the long-suffering peasantry. Having helped to put Madero in power, Zapata expected the new president to begin nationwide redistribution of the land. When Madero showed no inclination to overhaul the system of land ownership, Zapata rebelled against the new president, as he had rebelled against the old one.

Madero's more discerning supporters were appalled by his failure to destroy the power of the privileged class. It seemed to them that the Díaz regime remained intact, even though the old dictator was in exile. Madero's friends urged him to replace the thousands of government employees who were still loyal to Díaz, and to oust the Díaz-appointed generals who commanded the Mexican army. Instead of following this advice, Madero entrusted the defense of his government to Victoriano Huerta, a leading Díaz general. The president was to pay for that decision with his life.

Madero's rise to power had been made possible by the willingness of American officials to let him use the United States as his first base of operations, and to purchase the arms he needed to equip his troops. Madero's downfall was promoted by an American official, Henry Lane Wilson, who served as U.S. ambassador to Mexico during the latter part of the Díaz era and retained that post after Madero became president. The American ambassador believed that Mexicans needed strong-arm rule, and the disorder that developed after Díaz was forced from power frightened him. In fact, he demanded that the U.S. State Department send him 1,000 rifles and a million rounds of ammunition so that he could arm Americans and let them protect their extensive Mexican properties. He showed scant respect for Madero, whom he regarded as too weak to govern an essentially lawless country. In contrast, he openly admired Don Porfirio's nephew and other army officers who were plotting to overthrow the president.

Some historians, American as well as Mexican, regard Henry Lane Wilson as a co-conspirator in Madero's downfall, for he met in the U.S. embassy with the men who were plotting to depose Madero, and was aware of their plans. In 1913, when President Madero and Vice-President Pino Suárez were betrayed by Victoriano Huerta and imprisoned, the American ambassador did not protest. And when the president's wife and sister came to the embassy and begged the ambassador to save Madero's life, he refused to intervene.

The president and the vice-president of Mexico were murdered—a crime that was denounced by public officials and newspaper editors in the United States, Latin America, and Europe. The extent of the American ambassador's complicity in the assassination became the subject of debate in the United States. The controversial diplomat was recalled from his post. Having received a rebuke, Wilson resigned from the foreign service.

* * *

"He who sows the wind shall reap the whirlwind" is a Biblical expression that describes the later career of Victoriano Huerta. In ordering the assassination of President Madero and Vice-President Suárez, Huerta unleashed forces that swept Mexico like a hurricane. Madero's shortcomings were forgotten; he became the martyr of the revolution, and in death had more influence than he had possessed while living. In Madero's name, the enemies of the old order united to deprive Huerta of the spoils of office.

As head of the government, commander of the armed forces, and ally of the privileged class, Huerta enjoyed an initial advantage. And as he had already proved, he was willing to use violence to achieve his goals. A senator who was brave enough to describe Huerta as a cutthroat was taken to a cemetery and shot. That murder was the first in a series of assassinations that were meant to intimidate the legislature. Newspaper editors, labor leaders, and students who denounced Huerta as a usurper became targets for firing squads.

Huerta's opponents met violence with violence. To the south of Mexico City, Emiliano Zapata's peasant army fell upon the great haciendas owned by Huerta's supporters. The Zapatistas pillaged the mansions, burned the outbuildings, stole the best horses, and drove off the cattle. By the time Huerta's troops arrived at a ruined hacienda, Zapata and his men had vanished into the cane fields.

To the north, sometimes close to the American border, Francisco "Pancho" Villa waged deadly war against the Huerta army. As to whether Villa was a Mexican Robin Hood or a common bandit there was no agreement. What counted were the victories that his daring and his cunning brought about. His tactics were eminently suitable for the desert, where he usually fought. Surprise attacks were his specialty; he moved swiftly because his cavalry was well-mounted, and he commandeered freight trains to transport his foot soldiers and supplies. In the Villa army, the "*soldaderas*" played an important role. They were the soldiers' faithful women, who followed the army wherever it went, cooking for their men and nursing them when they were wounded.

Villa and Zapata were the best-known revolutionists because their exploits were dramatic. But almost every state in Mexico had its own "revolutionary army"—this was the proud name the guerrillas gave their ill-equipped, ill-disciplined forces.

As the guerrillas battled the regular army across Mexico, the country sank further into chaos. Thousands of civilians were killed, and hundreds of thousands were set adrift. Fields went unplowed and livestock untended. Churches

PANCHO VILLA LEADS HIS TROOPS TO WAR. Of all the leaders of the Mexican Revolution, Villa had the greatest hold on the popular imagination, American as well as Mexican. After his assassination, he became a folk hero. *The Bettmann Archive, Inc.*

were desecrated and robbed of their treasure; stores were stripped of their wares; factories shut down; mines ceased to operate; trains were dynamited and railroad tracks torn up. To finance their operations, both Huerta and the revolutionists forced rich people to "loan" them what silver and gold they were hoarding.

Mexico seemed bound for destruction. The revolution had taken a course of its own; men and women were no longer in control of events. One of the characters in Mariano Azuela's classic novel of the revolution, *The Underdogs,* described his countrymen's fate: "You ask me why I am still a rebel? Well, the revolution is like a hurricane: if you're in it, you're not a man . . . you're a leaf, a dead leaf, blown by the wind."

*   *   *

Huerta's enemies were not confined to Mexico. His most powerful opponent was Woodrow Wilson, President of the United States. Shortly after he was inaugurated in 1913, Wilson made it clear that he would never recognize Huerta as president of Mexico because he had overturned the lawful government. In withholding recognition, Wilson made it difficult for Huerta to buy the arms he needed to put down rebellion. Wilson hoped to force Huerta to relinquish the office that he had acquired by violent means; then the Mexican people could freely choose his successor. When Huerta did not yield to American pressure, President Wilson notified foreign governments that "if General Huerta does not retire by force of circumstances it will become the duty of the United States to use less peaceful means to put him out."

Wilson's warning was no idle threat, as two episodes famous in American diplomatic history shortly proved. In April, 1914, sailors from the *U.S.S. Dolphin* put ashore at Tampico, on the Gulf of Mexico, to load supplies for their ship. They were arrested and jailed because they had landed in a forbidden military zone. Shortly thereafter, the commanding officer in the Mexican port heard of the arrest, ordered the release of the American sailors, and sent an apology to their admiral. But the admiral took a grim view of the affair. He demanded that the Mexican naval command "publicly hoist the American flag in a prominent position on shore and salute it with 21 guns." The admiral gave Mexican officials 24 hours to comply with his ultimatum.

Huerta rejected the ultimatum, as head of the Mexican government. He pointed out that the American sailors had entered a forbidden zone, but after their arrest had promptly been released, and that the officer who had detained the Americans had been punished. Huerta then reminded President Wilson that the Treaty of Guadalupe Hidalgo, which had ended the 1846–1848 war between his country and the United States, provided for the peaceful settlement of disputes. He therefore offered to arbitrate the Tampico incident and other Mexican-American differences.

President Wilson was not willing to negotiate with a general whom he refused to recognize as president of Mexico. He ordered the Atlantic fleet into Mexican waters. Then he appeared before a joint session of Congress and asked its approval to use the armed forces of the United States to deal with the affront to their nation. A few days later, Wilson was informed that a German vessel was approaching Veracruz with a large shipment of arms for General Huerta.

President Wilson ordered the admiral of the Atlantic fleet to occupy the Mexican port to prevent the landing of the munitions. The U.S. Navy captured Veracruz in an engagement that cost the lives of more than 200 Mexicans, chiefly cadets of the Mexican naval academy, and the lives of 21 American sailors.

The occupation of Veracruz was a military and political disaster for Victoriano Huerta. Shortly thereafter, he gave up his office and went into exile in Europe. But the attack aroused anti-American feeling among all Mexicans, whatever their views on the revolution.

The Veracruz episode strengthened the position of Venustiano Carranza, the moderate leader who had declared himself "First Chief of the Constitutionalist Army." Although Carranza benefited from Huerta's ouster, he sent a sharp protest to the U.S. State Department, denouncing "the invasion of our territory" and the violation of "rights that constitute our existence as a free and independent sovereign entity." From that protest onward, Carranza challenged Woodrow Wilson's right to intervene in Mexican affairs.

*   *   *

Some historians balance their criticisms of Woodrow Wilson's high-handed dealings with Huerta with praise for the manner in which he restrained his countrymen from precipitating a war with Mexico after Carranza came to power. In 1914, many Americans felt that there was ample justification for sending the U.S. army across the border. American-owned mines, factories, railroads, and other property had been devastated during years of disorder. Hundreds of

American lives had been lost, the most outrageous killings having been the mass murder of 16 mining engineers by Pancho Villa. Public feeling had been inflamed by William Randolph Hearst, the owner of a chain of major newspapers in the United States—and the owner of much property in Mexico, including a million-acre ranch. The Hearst papers demanded "planting the American flag all the way to the Panama Canal."

Hostility to Mexicans, latent in the Southwest, became open as the result of the activities of Villa and other guerrilla leaders. So many Mexicans were killed on the American side of the border that *The New York Times* warned, "Too long have protests of the Mexican government against outrages upon its nationals in the border states fallen upon

VERACRUZ, 1914. In an effort to unseat General Huerta, whom he considered the illegal head of the Mexican government, President Wilson ordered the U.S. Navy to occupy the most important port in Mexico. *The Library of Congress*

deaf ears. . . . The killing of Mexicans without provocation is so common as to pass almost unnoticed."

Mexico and the United States were brought close to war in March, 1916, when Villa led a small army across the border and attacked Columbus, New Mexico. The village was sacked, and a number of Americans were killed. The next day, President Wilson ordered General John J. Pershing to lead a force of 6,000 into Mexico to capture Villa and his raiders. Venustiano Carranza, whom Wilson had grudgingly recognized as head of the Mexican government, bitterly assailed the American invasion. Instead of cooperating with General Pershing, as President Wilson had expected, Carranza's army obstructed the American effort to capture Villa. It was not until President Wilson ordered the withdrawal of the American army that the Carranza government moved against Villa and broke his power.

Wilson's decision to withdraw the American troops from Mexico was influenced by world events. The war that broke out in Europe in 1914 had by 1917 engulfed most of the world. It seemed inevitable that the United States would be drawn into the conflict. President Wilson recognized the danger that a hostile Mexico would present if the United States had to fight a war in Europe. That danger was underscored when the Zimmermann Note was made public in March, 1917. This famous communication, sent by the German foreign office to its ambassador in Mexico, was intercepted by British Naval Intelligence and brought to the attention of President Wilson. Arthur Zimmermann, the German foreign minister, was convinced that the United States would soon declare war on his country. He wanted to force the Americans to fight on a New World battlefront, which would undermine their war effort in Europe. Zimmermann therefore instructed his ambassador in Mexico to offer Carranza an alliance. With German support, the Mexican government would be encouraged to attack the United States and regain the territory that the Americans had taken in 1848.

Historians doubt that Carranza gave the German proposal serious consideration, but the disclosure of the Zimmermann Note served the Mexican leader's purpose. It brought him world attention, increased his prestige, and improved his chances of winning the approaching presidential election. Moreover, the United States became more conciliatory in its dealings with Carranza once it knew that the Germans were courting him.

Carranza had become the dominant figure in Mexican politics partly because he had not bent under the pressure exerted by Woodrow Wilson. The same tenacity of purpose served him well as he struggled with Villa, Zapata, and other guerrillas who threatened his government. But Carranza owed much to his generals, particularly to Álvaro Obregón, a rancher who had developed into a brilliant military strategist. One after another, Obregón defeated the generals who challenged Carranza. The head of state was thrown into eclipse by his dashing general.

But the threat that Álvaro Obregón posed did not become apparent for some time. Nineteen-seventeen was Carranza's year. A constitutional convention met that year under his sponsorship. Dominated by the more radical revolutionists, the convention gave Mexico the constitution that forms the basis of its present government. This fundamental law is sometimes described as the first "modern" constitution. Unlike the Constitution of the United States (1787), which dealt primarily with political relationships, such as the distribution of power between the state and national governments, the Mexican constitution of 1917 focused on the economic and social roles of government. For example, the constitution guaranteed the rights of labor, including the right to strike; provided for a system of public education; and severely restricted the nonreligious activities of the Church.

Several provisions of the new constitution eventually led to bitter conflict with the United States. One section reasserted an ancient principle: petroleum and other subsoil resources belonged to Mexico and could be exploited only under terms laid down by the national government. The surface area of Mexico, like the subsoil, was placed under the control of the national government, which thereafter had the power to redistribute land to both communities and individuals.

The 1917 constitution did not affect American interests for some years, because its provisions were largely ignored by Carranza, and his immediate successors did not openly challenge the foreign owners of Mexican mines and oil fields. In fact, Carranza, Obregón, and the other revolutionary leaders were too busy fighting one another to become involved in controversy with powerful foreign interests.

Events set in motion by Madero in 1908 followed a grim pattern for almost 30 years. Having overturned a president, the successful general assumed the highest civilian office, only to be driven from power by a rival general. And, in the hinterlands, lesser generals seized control of state governments, only to be ousted in short order. Few deposed governors or presidents died of natural causes; most were cut down by a firing squad or an assassin's bullet. Madero, Carranza, Villa, Zapata, Obregón, and scores of less famous revolutionists met death by assassination.

*   *   *

Mexico continued to be a violent land where soldiers owed allegiance to their general, rather than to their country, and where human life was little valued. But the rivalry of politically ambitious generals was not the only cause of violence. Some of the fiercest battles were fought in the name of religion. In the revolution that swept across Mexico, the Roman Catholic Church was a major victim. Fearing the political power of the clergy, and resenting the Church as the nation's greatest landowner, the revolutionists struck out: they stripped churches of their gold and silver, deprived convents of their sheep and cattle, and subjected the clergy to indignities. To make sure that the Church never again exerted undue influence in national affairs, the revolutionists placed provisions in the new constitution that separated church and state, and reduced the Church to something it had never been in Mexico—a purely religious organization.

The Mexican bishops decried what they regarded as the crippling provisions of the new constitution, and objected strenuously to the seizure of church property. But armed conflict between pro-Church and anti-Church factions did not occur on a nationwide basis until Plutarco Elías Calles became president in 1924. Calles and the clergy were soon locked in combat. The Catholic hierarchy denounced the 1917 constitution; Calles responded by activating anti-clerical provisions that hitherto had not been enforced. The number of priests who were allowed to officiate at religious services was limited. Religious instruction in primary schools was forbidden. Monasteries and convents were ordered to disband. Acts of worship could not be performed outside of churches. The clergy could not wear religious garb in public.

The Catholic hierarchy, backed by Pope Pius XI, reacted to the Calles edict by suspending religious services throughout Mexico. American Catholics joined their brethren throughout the world in condemning the policy of the Mexi-

THE CHURCH, A CENTRAL FACTOR. Although deprived of most of its economic and political power during the Mexican Revolution, the Roman Catholic Church remains an important force in determining social relations, such as family life.

Inter-American Development Bank

can president and in asking their government to take action. Mexican Catholics organized a boycott in an effort to paralyze the government, and set up organizations to defend their religion. The most militant of these groups adopted as its motto *"Viva Cristo Rey"*—"Long Live Christ the King." The Cristero movement had been born.

In defending the Church, Catholic militants resorted to some of the cruel practices of Villa and other guerrillas. In response, President Calles expelled the bishops from Mexico, closed Catholic schools and colleges, and deported foreign-born priests. Meanwhile, government troops gunned down Cristero guerrillas, or hanged them on telegraph poles as object lessons.

The religious war of the 1920s did not end with victory for either church or state. Instead, hostilities tapered off. President Calles and his supporters came to realize that in an overwhelmingly Catholic nation, even the most powerful government cannot suppress religion. For their part, Catholic leaders came to realize that the era in which the Church had enjoyed great economic and political power was at an end.

In 1927, the President of the United States, Calvin Coolidge, indirectly influenced church–state relations in Mexico. To serve as his ambassador to one of the most socialistic nations in the world, Coolidge named a partner in a great international banking house—an institution that had become the very symbol of capitalism. But Dwight Morrow of J. P. Morgan & Company established excellent rapport with President Calles. Ambassador Morrow eased the tension that had developed in Mexican-American relations when the Calles government had begun to enforce provisions of the 1917 constitution that affected foreign-owned property. The American ambassador also influenced President Calles to adopt a more conciliatory policy toward the Church.

* * *

For years the people of the United States were frightened, angered, and grieved in turn as they watched developments in the Mexican Revolution. But after Álvaro Obregón became president in 1920, Americans became aware of an amazing development in the neighboring republic. Mexico was in the throes of a new kind of revolution, one in which the participants were not soldiers but educators, painters, musicians, anthropologists, writers, and archeologists.

After centuries of rejecting their Indian heritage, Mexicans were learning to be proud of it. Subsidized by the government, archeologists uncovered stupendous cities and religious centers that had been ancient when the Spaniards arrived in the New World. José Vasconcelos, the learned and dynamic minister of education in the Obregón administration, inspired Mexican students with his missionary zeal and sent them to remote villages to teach Indians. Vasconcelos also invited Mexican artists to paint murals on the walls of public buildings. Diego Rivera, José Clemente Orozco, and David Alfaro Siqueiros—all of them revolutionists and all of them pro-Indian—were soon attracting crowds to admire their monumental works.

American critics, impressed by the music, art, and writing of the revolutionary generation, now spoke of the Mexican Renaissance. Mexico, long the mecca of Americans who wanted to exploit the resources of their neighbor nation, now attracted visitors who came to admire and to learn. The flow of American tourists began as a trickle, even before the military phase of revolution ended in the 1920s. With peace, the number of tourists increased to a flood. Money spent by visiting Americans became a mainstay of the Mexican economy. And as hundreds of thousands of Americans visited Mexico each year to see its natural and man-made wonders, the Rio Grande became less significant as a cultural boundary.

9

Black Gold, White Hope

The drill bored almost two miles below the ocean floor before it tapped the pocket of oil and gas. Suddenly there was an eruption as immense pressure forced oil and gas upward through the casing of the well. The pipes and valves designed to control the flow of oil were blown apart. As oil gushed from the ocean floor, the sea around the drilling rig seemed to boil. Gas ignited and formed a fireball above the oil, making it appear that the Gulf of Mexico was ablaze. The worst oil spill in history had been started.

Ixtoc I, the name of the runaway well, was soon famous, and its location off the Mexican coast appeared on maps in newspapers for the next nine months. Reporters, photographers, and television crews kept the world abreast of developments as experts from Mex.co and the United States struggled to bring the blowout under control. Meanwhile, Ixtoc I spewed more than 400,000 gallons of oil each day, creating a vast slick that moved across the Gulf of Mexico and threatened Texas beaches.

Pemex (Petróleos Mexicanos), the oil monopoly of the Mexican government, owned the well, but the drilling had been done by a Mexican company using equipment leased from Americans. The three parties affected by the blowout cooperated in an effort to cap the well. More than 100,000 metal balls were injected into the surging oil to decrease the flow. Next, a huge cone was suspended over the well to catch as much oil as possible and pump it into anchored barges. Meanwhile, relief wells were bored at an angle on either side of the blowout to tap the flow. Ixtoc I went out of control in June, 1979; it was not capped until March, 1980, by which time it had spilled more than 120 *million* gallons of oil into the Gulf of Mexico. The Mexican drilling contractor spent more than $200 million in bringing Ixtoc I under control. But that was not the end of his troubles. A year later, the United States government sued the Mexican company to recover the cost of cleaning up Texas beaches affected by the oil spill. In addition, the United States demanded payment for damages to fish and other natural resources within its coastal waters.

The runaway oil well was the cause of sharp diplomatic exchanges between the governments of Mexico and the United States. At the same time, Ixtoc I was the cause of considerable satisfaction to Mexican officials. It was a test well that had been drilled beneath the shallow waters of the Bay of Campeche in a search for offshore oil deposits. The productivity of Ixtoc I and other wells drilled nearby exceeded all expectations. Petroleum experts, who had estimated Mexico's proven oil reserves at 6 billion barrels in 1976, only four years later raised the figure to 60 billion barrels, thanks to the discovery of new oil fields in the Bay of Campeche and other areas of the Gulf coast. Mexico assumed new importance in international affairs when petroleum engineers compared its oil potential with that of Saudi Arabia, the world's leading producer.

American officials, conscious of their country's dependence upon imported oil, recognized the significance of Mexico's rapidly expanding petroleum resources. From every point of view, importing oil from Mexico was preferable to importing oil from the Middle East. But Mexico, now among the most courted of all nations, made it clear that in exporting oil, its policy would be determined by its own national interest, rather than by the needs of its powerful neighbor. In other words, relations between the two nations had changed radically since 1901, when an American drilled the first oil well near Tampico and thus began an era when foreigners exploited Mexican oil for their own benefit.

*　　*　　*

Mexico became a new kind of battleground during the last years of the Díaz era (1900–1911). In their efforts to find and remove the "black gold" trapped far below the surface of the earth, American and European oil developers waged ruthless war in Mexico, sometimes with bullets, but more often with sharp business practices, including bribes and forged bills of sale. Their incentive was the rapid expansion of the market for petroleum brought on by the mass production of automobiles, and by the conversion of locomotives and battleships from coal-burning to oil-burning engines.

An American, Edward L. Doheny, was the most enterprising of a group of developers who came to be known as the oil barons of Mexico. While he was still in his 20s, Doheny was a successful silver prospector in the southwestern United States. After moving to California, he drilled a number of productive oil wells. The railroad executive who bought Doheny's oil for his locomotives later became president of the Mexican Central, an American-owned railway. At his countryman's suggestion, Doheny began prospecting for oil along the Gulf coast of Mexico near Tampico.

Doheny and his partner slashed through the jungle for weeks before they found what they were looking for: oil oozing out of the ground. The two Americans used their own funds and money borrowed from the Mexican Central Railroad to lease or buy more than 700 square miles of land adjacent to the oil seepage. Their object was to exclude competition from what they expected to develop into the richest oil field in the world. But a British engineer got wind of American activity in the Tampico area, and he assembled an extensive tract of land adjoining the American stake.

The oil boom that developed in the Tampico region was like the gold rush that had transformed California 50 years before. Thousands of oil prospectors converged on the Gulf coast of Mexico. Tampico became a wild, lawless town overrun by foreigners. In exploiting their newfound treasure, the American and European oil barons abused Mexican resources and misused the Mexican people. Frequently a foreigner's title to the land was fraudulent. Rightful owners who were driven from their land generally had no recourse, because local police were often in the pay of the foreign oilmen.

The stakes got even higher when first the British and then the Americans brought in gushers—wells that literally exploded oil. Pipelines and railroads were built through the jungle to bring oil to the tankers waiting in the harbor at Tampico. To protect what they already had, and to improve their chances of getting more, the oil barons moved from bribing local officials to bribing generals, governors, and presidents. It was not only Mexican officials who were corrupted—the land itself was damaged, sometimes irreparably. One gusher caught fire and burned for 40 days; another killed thousands of cattle by spraying their pastures with oil. The uncontrolled oil then ran into the sea, contaminating 300 miles of coastline. Meanwhile, the Mexican workers who enabled foreigners to enrich themselves were underpaid and overworked by the American and European corporations that had bought the properties developed by the oil barons.

When the Mexican Revolution began and Porfirio Díaz fell from power, some Mexicans believed that their government would gain control of the oil fields. They soon discovered that the foreigners' grip on the oil industry was as firm under Madero, Huerta, and Carranza as it had been in the days of Don Porfirio. Many factions were struggling to control Mexico, and all of them were in desperate need of money. The British and American oil companies were an ever-ready source of funds for generals who promised to protect the rights of foreigners. Moreover, the outbreak of World War I strengthened the position of the oil companies. The British were in particular need of Mexican oil for their navy, which at that time controlled the seas. The British government could be counted upon to protect the companies that provided fuel for its battleships.

Mexicans who rejected the idea that foreigners had the right to monopolize the oil resources of their country looked forward to the day when Mexico would be strong enough to gain control of its national treasure. Among these Mexicans was a young officer who had been stationed near Tampico during the early stages of the revolution. He had observed the operation of the foreign-controlled oil industry and had been outraged by what he saw.

* * *

Lázaro Cárdenas, who is now a national hero, was a soldier in the Mexican Revolution while he was still in his teens, and at the age of 25 became the youngest general in the Mexican army. But he was not a typical general: he never shot his prisoners, and he did not enrich himself. In 1928, as the military phase of the revolution was ending, Cárdenas was elected governor of his native state, Michoacán. His administration attracted national attention because he built schools and roads, launched irrigation and flood-control projects, and distributed land to peasants.

Six years after his election as governor of Michoacán,

Cárdenas became president of Mexico. His elevation to that high office was only partly due to his military career and his success as governor. More importantly, Cárdenas was the protégé of Plutarco Elías Calles, the strong man of Mexico.

Calles was a schoolteacher who became a leading general during the revolution; as we saw in the last chapter, he moved from that position to the presidency. After leaving office, Calles increased his already formidable power by organizing the National Revolutionary Party in 1929. In that new political grouping, Calles brought together the leaders of the principal interest groups in Mexico: the military, labor, agriculture, business, and industry. The National Revolutionary Party was a means of forcing rival groups to compromise, instead of resorting to civil war. The organization changed its name to the Party of the Mexican Revolution, and finally to the Institutional Revolutionary Party—popularly known as PRI. Despite the changes in its name, the party objective remained the same: to provide continuity and structure for revolutionary change.

From the day of its organization until the present, PRI has remained the official party and the dominating influence in Mexican politics. In fact, the only route to political advancement is through PRI. Every president since Calles has been a member of PRI, and so have nearly all governors, members of the state and national legislatures, and judges at all levels of government. Other political parties do exist, but they have few members and control only those offices that PRI allots them as token opposition. To all intents and purposes, Mexico has a one-party political system.

Since it enjoys a virtual monopoly of political power, PRI is very different from the Democratic and Republican parties of the United States, which are loosely organized, rather evenly matched groups that compete for public office. Whereas the national chairmen of the two major parties in the United States primarily raise money and coordinate campaigns, the head of PRI has a major role in the selection of candidates and in determining policy. He is one of the most powerful of all Mexicans.

When Lázaro Cárdenas became head of the official party in 1930, he was in a position to influence the course of the revolution, which had ceased to be military in character. The term now meant socioeconomic change. He believed that the goals of the revolution had been forgotten by Calles as he grew older, richer, and more conservative. But, with Calles' blessing, Cárdenas was nominated for the presidential term 1934–1940.

In Mexico, each president chooses his successor, and his choice is automatically ratified by the official party. The PRI candidate actually needs to do little campaigning, since his election is assured. But Cárdenas, like most of his successors, campaigned across Mexico like an American presidential candidate. When he assumed office, he was the best-known incoming president that Mexico had ever had. It soon became apparent that Cárdenas intended to activate the stalled economic and social revolution. He had the authority to do so, because the president of Mexico answers neither to congress nor to the courts. During his six-year term of office, he can wield almost dictatorial power if he chooses. Cárdenas removed the followers of ex-president

Calles from his government, and, having assured himself that the army was loyal, he forced the former strong man into exile in the United States so that he could not obstruct the next phase of the revolution.

In fulfilling what he regarded as the promises made in the constitution of 1917, Cárdenas came into conflict with the United States. He redistributed more land than all his predecessors combined. Some of the land that Cárdenas took had belonged to American citizens. While the United States recognized the Mexican government's right to expropriate the land of foreign owners, it insisted that a fair price be paid for the property. But the Mexican government and the landowners seldom agreed on the value of the expropriated property, and the foreigners wanted to be paid in cash, while the Mexican government offered its bonds. In some instances, the Cárdenas administration challenged the foreigners' rights to certain properties on the grounds that they had been acquired illegally. Payment for the expropriated property of American citizens was the subject of protracted negotiations between Mexico and the United States. The issue was never resolved to the satisfaction of some of the Americans involved.

*   *   *

The expropriation of foreign-owned agricultural lands strained relations between Mexico and the United States. But the expropriation of foreign-owned oil fields brought relations between Mexico and the United States to the crisis stage.

Mexican labor unions became more militant after Cárdenas became president. The oil-field workers demonstrated that militancy when they challenged their employers—the American and European companies that controlled the Mexican petroleum industry. In 1937, the union of oil-field workers demanded a sharp increase in wages, along with improved living and working conditions. The oil companies rejected the demands, and the union leaders called a strike.

The conflict between the native workers and the foreign owners exposed Mexican bitterness toward the giant oil companies. It was widely believed that the foreign corporations had acquired many of their holdings illegally, and that they paid minimal taxes and placed themselves above Mexican law because they counted on the backing of their own governments.

Cárdenas regarded the impending oil workers' strike as a disaster. The Mexican economy, already weakened by decades of civil war and by the cost of land redistribution, was feeling the effects of a worldwide economic depression. A work stoppage in a major industry would make a bad situation worse. For that reason, the president persuaded the union to submit its dispute to arbitration. The board of arbitration recommended a wage increase smaller than the one demanded by the union, but at length the workers accepted the recommendation.

The oil companies rejected the compromise and took their case to the supreme court of Mexico. The high court ruled against the oil companies and set a date for their compliance with the decision of the board of arbitration. The oil companies announced that they would ignore the supreme court ruling. Then they challenged the Mexican government by taking out full-page advertisements in leading newspapers to defend their rejection of the supreme court ruling. At the international level, the oil companies refused to buy and market Mexican oil and called on their own governments to exert pressure on President Cárdenas.

The president met with his cabinet to decide upon a course of action. At the end of the meeting, he addressed the people of his nation on a radio hookup. The president explained that the foreign oil companies, forgetting that they had placed themselves under Mexican law when they chose to exploit the resources of the host country, had defied the sovereignty of the nation. The Mexican government would respond to this challenge to its authority by transferring the ownership of the oil fields, pipelines, and refineries from the foreign companies to the Mexican people. In other words, the foreign-owned companies were to be nationalized. The president warned his listeners that the cost would be staggering. To pay the foreign companies for their property would impose a heavy burden on every Mexican.

In response to the nationalization of the oil companies, the British government broke off diplomatic relations with Mexico, and the United States halted its purchases of Mexican silver. But Cárdenas proceeded with his plans in the belief that conditions at home and abroad were in his favor. The Mexican people, including the Catholic hierarchy, gave the president overwhelming support. Impending war in Europe made the British unwilling to intervene in Mexican affairs. The president of the United States, Franklin D. Roosevelt, had developed the Good Neighbor Policy in dealing

THE PRESIDENT RALLIES HIS PEOPLE. When President Cárdenas announced on a nationwide radio hookup that his government had decided to nationalize the foreign-owned oil industry, he received the overwhelming support of the Mexican people.

Wide World Photos

with Latin American nations. Non-intervention in the domestic affairs of other New World countries was a major principle of Roosevelt's policy. Backing the oil companies in their dispute with Mexico would jeopardize the friendly relations that the United States had established with all the Latin American republics. At the urging of the Roosevelt

173

administration, the oil companies entered into negotiations with the Mexican government for the purchase of their enormous holdings.

*　　*　　*

A government monopoly, Petróleos Mexicanos (Pemex), replaced the foreign oil companies. Today, Pemex searches for oil and gas deposits, drills wells, builds pipelines, operates refineries, and sells gasoline. Pemex has developed one of the world's largest petrochemical industries, and it converts petroleum into a wide variety of products. The director of Pemex not only has great influence over Mexican economic policy; he exercises political power as well, because the connections between government and industry are far closer in Mexico than in the United States. Though all phases of American commerce and industry are subject to extensive government regulation, ownership remains overwhelmingly private. In contrast, the Mexican government owns or partially owns a number of key industries, and dictates policy in many others.

The redistribution of land, the development of extensive irrigation projects, and the establishment of banks for farmers gave the Mexican government dominant influence in agriculture in the 1920s. About 90 percent of the electric power now generated in Mexico is produced by government installations, and a large percentage of the national output of iron and steel, automobiles, textiles, and electrical goods is manufactured by government-owned facilities. The Mexican government has a virtual monopoly on communications and transportation systems, while the Bank of Mexico and a large number of specialized banks give the government further control over the economy.

Although the United States and other foreign countries have been excluded from a large part of the Mexican economy, Americans have increased their hold on business and industry in their neighbor nation in recent years. The oil industry is an example. A large part of the equipment used by Pemex is American-made. In 1979, the year that Ixtoc I went out of control, Pemex bought equipment valued at $205 million in the United States. For the period 1980–1985, the Pemex budget has been set at $12 billion. Much of that sum will be spent in the United States. Pemex also employs thousands of Americans as consultants and technicians.

It is not just government-owned industries that buy equipment in the United States. Privately owned steelworks, textile mills, and other business concerns purchase quantities of machinery, electric and electronic equipment, precision instruments, and chemicals from American companies. And since, in recent years, Mexico has not produced enough grain to feed its people, it buys thousands of tons of American wheat and corn. In 1980 alone, Mexico paid almost $2 billion for food imported from the United States. Altogether, more than 60 percent of all Mexican imports comes from the United States.

American companies not only export their products to Mexico—they also produce goods within that country. More than 500 American companies operate in Mexico under the Border Industrialization Plan, which was established by the Mexican government to provide employment for its citizens.

The plan operates in a duty-free zone along the Mexican border with the United States. Foreign companies bring parts and materials to Mexico with the guarantee that they will be assembled within the duty-free zone. If the finished product is exported, the Mexican government collects no customs duties on the materials that were brought into the country from the United States or other foreign country. If a finished product, such as a suit of clothes or a pocket calculator, is returned to the country where the parts were manufactured, customs officials collect duties only on the value added by assembling the article. Quantities of clothing, electronic devices, and other products that require a great deal of hand labor are now assembled in Mexico and exported to the United States. The Border Industrialization Plan has thrived, despite the protests of American labor leaders, who oppose "runaway" businesses (that is, businesses that move their operations out of the United States in order to make use of cheap labor in Mexico).

Although the Mexican government monopolizes certain key industries, it provides a favorable climate for individual businessmen and public corporations, both native and foreign. Low taxes, investment incentives, subsidized prices for raw materials, and wage controls all favor business enterprise. According to a leading political economist, Roger D. Hansen of Johns Hopkins University, "It is difficult to imagine a combination of policies aimed at rewarding the activity of private businessmen more than the policies established by the Mexican government after 1940."

American corporations have taken advantage of the inducements offered by the Mexican government to make heavy investments in a number of industries. Because of laws designed to prevent foreign companies from controlling Mexican industry, American corporations often form partnerships with Mexican capitalists. A recent listing showed almost 500 joint ventures between Mexican industrialists and foreign companies, most of them based in the United States. American corporate investments in Mexico, concentrated in manufacturing, now exceed $4 billion.

The close association between Mexican and American corporations has its critics on both sides of the border. Some economists maintain that the system of joint ownership gives American corporations undue control over Mexican industry and increases Mexican dependence on the United States for technology and financing. Some labor leaders regard the arrangement as an effort on the part of American corporations to "export" jobs to a country that has a low wage scale.

Corporations based in the United States exercise great influence over the Mexican economy because they build factories, introduce new technology, hire workers, and sell their products in the Mexican market. American banks also have great leverage, because they lend money to Mexican companies and public agencies. Banks with headquarters in the United States now carry more than $11 billion in outstanding loans and credits extended to Mexican borrowers—a circumstance that makes the debtor nation economically dependent.

The American influence over the Mexican economy is manifested in yet other ways. More than 70 percent of all Mexican exports goes to the United States. Oil, natural gas, minerals, winter vegetables, and shrimp are important exports to the United States. Mexican leaders sometimes point out that their country has a colonial type of economy, because it exports raw materials to the United States and imports manufactured products.

Mexico imports far more from the United States than it exports to its neighbor. To help offset its unfavorable trade balance, Mexico relies upon the money sent home by its migrant workers in the United States. Even more important to the Mexican economy are the expenditures of tourists, including thousands of retired Americans who live in Mexico during all or part of the year. In 1980, more than four million tourists, most of them Americans, visited Mexico. By promoting tourism and by encouraging the construction of hotels and recreational facilities, the Mexican government hopes to have eight million tourists each year by 1985. The national tourist plan recently drawn up showed that earnings from tourism increased from less than $500 million in 1970 to well over $1 billion ten years later. The goal for 1985 has been set at $3.5 billion in revenue from tourism. In short, the money spent by American tourists is vital to the Mexican economy, because it helps to pay for the goods and services that Mexico buys from the United States.

Since the United States is by far Mexico's most important trading partner, Mexico is vulnerable to economic conditions north of the Rio Grande. A recession in the United States has damaging repercussions in Mexico. The number of American tourists declines sharply; migrant workers in the United States lose their jobs and return to their home country; the market for Mexican shrimp and winter vegetables is curtailed; American industries reduce their imports of Mexican minerals.

In recent years, the Mexican government has attempted to lessen its dependence upon the American economy by expanding its trade with Europe and Japan. But, while some progress has been made in that direction, the United States remains the chief market for Mexican goods and services. Moreover, trade between Mexico and the United States is expanding rapidly. Trade levels almost tripled in the period 1977–1980: Mexican-American trade exceeded $25 billion in 1980, as compared with $9 billion in 1977. Mexico now ranks as the third largest trading partner of the United States, and some economists predict that in the near future

"SOWING THE OIL." As millions of Mexicans move from rural to urban areas, shantytowns grow on the outskirts of cities. With revenue derived from oil and gas exports, the Mexican government now assists many of its citizens to replace the shacks they once occupied with substantial houses such as these.

Inter-American Development Bank

Mexico will move ahead of Canada and Japan to first position.

The enormous economic influence that the United States exerts over Mexico is equaled by its cultural influence. For many years, American motion pictures and television programs, American books and magazines, American sports and popular music—even American slang—have had an impact south of the Rio Grande. The cultural and economic influence of the United States is resented by many Mexicans, who refer to their neighbor as "the Colossus of the North." They sometimes describe the overpowering presence of the United States as a form of imperialism. In other words, the economic and cultural power of its neighbor prevents Mexico from being truly independent.

But in 1980, as engineers continued their upward revision of proven petroleum reserves of Mexico, many Americans began to view their southern neighbor with new interest and respect. Businessmen and statesmen alike were impressed when the Central Intelligence Agency estimated that Mexico could export as much as five million barrels of oil per day by 1985, if it chose. Such a figure represented a major part of the import needs of the United States. That potential gave Mexico powerful leverage in its dealings with the United States.

10

"Doomed to Be Neighbors"

When the captain saw a plane circling his boat, he knew that he was in for trouble. Until that moment, it had been a good trip. Three days after putting out from San Diego, he had sighted a school of tuna, the biggest he had ever found. His crew sprang to action; the seine was dropped overboard, and as the net played out behind the ship, the big fish began to strike it. In half the usual time, the net was filled, emptied, and spread again.

The plane dipped low enough for the captain to see the Mexican colors on the fuselage. He knew that the patrol had spotted the American flag on his boat.

Before leaving San Diego, the captain had heard that the Mexican authorities were threatening to seize foreign tuna boats that fished within 200 miles of their coast, but he'd decided to take the risk. The waters off the Mexican coast provided some of the best tuna fishing in the world.

Several hours after the plane circled the fishermen, a gunboat flying the Mexican flag hove into sight. As the armed vessel came alongside the tuna boat, an officer, in polite and perfect English, ordered the American captain to turn his boat around and put in at the nearest Mexican port.

The "tuna war" between Mexico and the United States began that July afternoon in 1980. During the next week, six American boats were seized, their cargoes confiscated, and each owner forced to pay a fine of $13,330 before his boat was released. The news quickly spread to all the American tuna boats plying Mexican waters. To avoid seizure, the captains headed their boats for San Diego. The American tuna fleet was idled, and bankruptcy faced the owners.

The United States government protested the seizure of the property of its citizens, and declared that the Mexican action was unlawful. Like Mexico, the United States claimed rights to natural resources within a 200-mile-wide "exclusive economic zone" off its coasts. But, since tuna are migratory fish, the U.S. State Department contended that they were exempt from the control of any nation.

President López Portillo rejected the U.S. State Department's interpretation of international law and referred to the American boats as pirate ships. The "tuna war" escalated. The United States banned all imports of Mexican tuna, and denied Mexican fishing boats the right to catch squid off the New England coast. In retaliation, Mexico terminated all its fishing treaties with the United States.

The ill-feeling created by the "tuna war" made negotiations between Mexico and the United States difficult. The Mexicans were bitter about what they regarded as another example of the Americans' high-handed treatment of a weaker nation. For decades, the American fishing fleet had made lucrative hauls from Mexican waters. In an effort to benefit from its own natural resources, the Mexican government had adopted a new policy in 1976. Between that year and 1980, hundreds of millions of dollars were invested in fishing boats and onshore facilities for processing their catch. Having spent so much money, the Mexican government attempted to protect its investment by prohibiting foreigners from taking tuna in its territorial waters.

*　　*　　*

The Mexican government's effort to increase the annual catch of fish from 600,000 tons to 2.4 million tons in the decade 1976–1986 was one phase of an ambitious program for expanding the production of every type of food, from the land as well as from the ocean. Once an exporter of grain, Mexico began to import that essential food in the 1970s, when production failed to keep pace with population growth. In 1980, Mexico had to import more than 10 million tons of wheat and corn, and most of it came from the United States.

As food imports soared, Mexican officials realized that their country had become vulnerable to pressure from the United States, its chief supplier. In fact, several officials expressed the fear that the United States might wield its "food weapon" against Mexico as it had recently used that coercive measure against the Soviet Union. More specifically, at some future time the American government might demand an increase in the amount of oil delivered to the United States as the price for permission to buy food. The "oil weapon," which some Mexicans counted on to provide a measure of equality in their dealings with the United States, would be useless as long as their country was dependent upon imported food.

In an effort to make his country self-sufficient in food production, President López Portillo stressed the modernization of agriculture. Revenue derived from the sale of petroleum and natural gas was channeled into the campaign for raising food production—a program known as "sowing the oil." To bring arid areas under irrigation, rivers were dammed and deep wells were sunk. In southeastern Mexico, where rainfall is ample but much of the land is low-lying, extensive drainage projects added to the area under cultivation. By making loans for machinery, and by providing the advice of agricultural experts, the government helped many landowners to convert from subsistence farming to more productive agriculture.

But "sowing the oil" meant more than overhauling Mexican agriculture. Funds were also used for building roads, improving schools, extending power lines, and constructing low-cost housing. A principal object of the program was to improve the living standards of rural people and thus discourage them from migrating. But the chances of keeping rural people where they presently live appear slim, in the opinion of many observers. For agriculture to be efficient, small farms must be combined into larger holdings so that machinery may be used to advantage. Fewer farmers are required when large-scale agriculture is practiced, which means that inevitably many rural Mexicans will be "tractored" off the land, as one farmer described it.

*   *   *

If it succeeds, the campaign to achieve self-sufficiency in food production will make Mexico less vulnerable to one form of pressure from the United States. But in modernizing agriculture, Mexican officials are making their country even more subject to another kind of American pressure: the pressure to curtail illegal immigration. The thousands of rural families that are forced from the land each year either join their relatives in overcrowded Mexican cities or migrate to the United States, swelling the ranks of illegal aliens.

As we have seen, illegal migration to the United States has become a way of life for hundreds of thousands of Mexicans. For the Mexican government, this constant movement across the border has become an economic necessity. As a consequence, recent proposals for drastic changes in American immigration policy alarm Mexican officials.

A national public-opinion poll conducted by the Roper organization in 1977 showed that 91 percent of the American people wanted stricter enforcement of immigration laws. From that time on, the problem of illegal immigration has been widely debated in the nation's press. Since far more undocumented aliens enter the United States from Mexico than from any other country, illegal migrants from that nation have been the major focus of attention.

In a recent statement in *The New York Times,* Roger

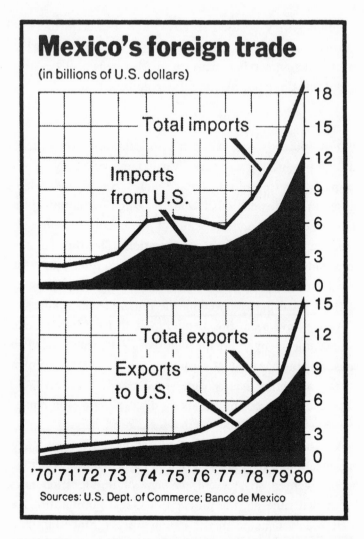

Mexico's foreign trade

(in billions of U.S. dollars)

Total imports

Imports from U.S.

18
15
12
9
6
3
0

Total exports

Exports to U.S.

15
12
9
6
3
0

'70 '71 '72 '73 '74 '75 '76 '77 '78 '79 '80

Sources: U.S. Dept. of Commerce; Banco de Mexico

EXPANDING TRADE. Trade between Mexico and the United States has increased sharply in recent years. Some economists predict that Mexico will move past Canada and Japan to become the number one trading partner of the United States.

Copyright © 1981 by the New York Times Company. Reprinted by permission

Conner of the Federation for American Immigration Reform (FAIR) maintained that some employers took advantage of their competitors by hiring illegal immigrants at rates below the minimum wage. Moreover, he said, the employment of undocumented aliens deprived American workers of jobs, and weakened labor unions because illegal immigrants were afraid to join for fear of revealing their unlawful status. As we saw earlier in this book, Conner's view of the undocumented worker is shared by a number of Americans.

Hamilton Fish, Jr., a member of the House of Representatives subcommittee that deals with immigration policy, viewed undocumented aliens from a somewhat different angle. Fish said that it was ironic that Congress spent so much time setting quotas on the number of *legal* immigrants to be admitted to the United States while "the back door is open and as many people or more are coming in on their own initiative as are coming in legally through the Immigration and Naturalization Service." A recent editorial in the liberal magazine *The New Republic* reinforced the point made by the congressman. It called attention to the fact that more than a million applicants for immigration visas, many of them with relatives in the United States, were blocked at American consular offices around the world. The editorial questioned the fairness of a system that denied entry to qualified immigrants while permitting undocumented aliens to enter at will.

* * *

President John F. Kennedy once referred to the United States as a nation of immigrants to remind his listeners that, with the exception of American Indians, the people of the nation are all the descendants of aliens. The idea of the United States as a melting pot is firmly established; until recently, few Americans doubted that their country could assimilate an endless number of immigrants. But the integration of millions of Mexican immigrants into American society has proved exceptionally difficult, in the opinion of some observers. The sheer number of Mexican aliens, most of whom have entered illegally, is the most obvious reason for assimilation problems. The proximity of their native country and the ease with which they can move back and forth across the border discourages undocumented Mexicans from putting down roots in the United States. Interviews conducted by Mexican and American researchers indicate that most illegal immigrants regard themselves as temporary workers, rather than potential citizens.

Mexican immigrants do not have to learn English when they come to the United States. They can settle in communities where Spanish is universally spoken; Spanish-language movies, radio broadcasts, and television shows are accessible to them; and when they attend church, services are conducted in their native language. Since undocumented Mexicans are often the victims of discrimination, they are likely to develop a group identity that makes assimilation difficult. Some Chicano organizations have promoted the feeling of group identity by encouraging the use of the Spanish language and the perpetuation of Mexican culture.

It is true that Mexican-American leaders also stress the importance of learning English. They insist that if young Americans of Mexican origin are to compete for jobs and get beyond the inferior economic status in which many members of their group are presently trapped, they must master the working language of the country in which they live. But teaching children of Mexican birth to speak English is a formidable undertaking for the nation's schools. In 1980, the U.S. Department of Education estimated that 3.5 million children who spoke no English were living in the United States. Three out of four of those children were of Hispanic origin. Merely providing buildings and teachers for all these children posed serious problems for local and state boards of education. To complicate the problem, sharp disagreement has developed over the proper way to teach non-English-speaking children.

Until recent years, most immigrant children learned English by being forced to attend schools where they heard no other language. For many young aliens, schooling was a bitter experience. The civil rights movement of the 1960s effected changes in the traditional method of educating foreign-born children. Chicano organizations played a major role in the introduction of the bilingual method of teaching children whose "home" language was Spanish. Vilma Martínez, president and general counsel of the Mexican-American Legal Defense and Educational Fund, described the method when she said, "We believe the best-quality program for Mexican Americans is bilingual education—the use of the child's own language to teach the child English."

The bilingual method of teaching requires the employment of teachers who are fluent in both English and the pupils' home language. Children are taught English, mathematics, social studies, and other subjects in their home language.

Only when they know English well enough to cope with instruction in that language are they placed in classes with pupils whose native tongue is English.

Bilingual education has aroused opposition from the outset. Critics object to the cost and the difficulty of administering what they describe as a dual system of education. They believe that bilingual education perpetuates the use of their native language by a large and growing minority—an undesirable situation from both a social and political standpoint. Opponents of the system are disturbed at the prospect of future problems similar to those posed by the French-speaking minority in Canada.

Many critics of bilingual education insist that English should be taught by the direct, or "total immersion," method. With this method, non-English-speaking children are brought together in one classroom, whatever their home language may be. They are taught by an instructor trained in the "English as a second language" method. Throughout the school day the child is exposed to nothing but skillfully taught English, and the teacher's goal is to make pupils *think* in English as well as to acquire a vocabulary. In other words, the object is to have children learn a second language the way they learned their first language as infants.

In the 1960s pressure from Chicano groups and civil rights organizations induced local school boards in the Southwestern states to introduce bilingual education for Mexican-American students. State legislatures, in some instances because of court rulings, provided money to supplement local budgets for the new system of instruction. In 1967, Congress appropriated funds to subsidize bilingual education in schools where non-English-speaking children were concentrated, and the U.S. Department of Education established guidelines for administering the program. By 1980, the annual federal expenditure for bilingual education had reached almost $200 million.

Federal support for bilingual education was drastically curtailed by the Reagan administration. Shortly after his inauguration, President Reagan directed his secretary of education to withdraw proposed regulations that would have required public schools to teach non-English-speaking pupils in their native language. In obeying the president's directive, the secretary of education charged that the rules projected by the previous administration had been "harsh, inflexible, unworkable, and incredibly costly." In defending his decision to change federal policy, President Reagan offered this reason for his action: "It is absolutely wrong and against American concepts to have a bilingual program that is now openly, admittedly dedicated to preserving their native language and never getting them adequate in English so they can go out into the job market."

The new federal policy met with wide approval by local school boards in some parts of the Southwest. But Hispanic-American leaders deplored the curtailment of federal support. Edward R. Roybal, a Democratic congressman from California, declared that the president's move would deprive millions of children of their civil rights. The policy change made by the Reagan administration was widely reported in Mexican newspapers, particularly those in the larger cities. Some editorials interpreted the president's decision as harmful to relations between the neighboring republics. But the attention of Mexican editors was soon diverted from bilingual education to a more compelling issue.

* * *

Shortly after President Reagan announced his decision on bilingual education, a commission authorized by Congress to review immigration policy made its historic report. The panel consisted of eight members of Congress, four people who had been in President Carter's cabinet, and four members chosen from the public at large—one of whom, the Reverend Theodore Hesburgh, president of the University of Notre Dame, was the chairman of the commission. Congress established the commission in 1978 and instructed it to report its findings by March 1, 1981. The panel conducted interviews and public hearings, collected data, and appraised official immigration policy before making its recommendations.

The long-awaited report attracted considerable attention on both sides of the Rio Grande, because much of it pertained to Mexican immigration to the United States. For example, the commission reported that the Border Patrol was so undermanned and so ill-equipped that it was virtually powerless to halt the flow of undocumented Mexicans. And since the Immigration and Naturalization Service lacked computers and other devices for keeping tabs on aliens who entered the United States as students or visitors, many of them remained in this country after their visas expired.

The commission described the adverse effects of illegal immigration on American life. "This illegal flow, encouraged by employers who provide jobs, has created an underclass of workers who fear apprehension and deportation. Undocumented, illegal migrants, at the mercy of unscrupulous employers and 'coyotes' who smuggle them across the border, cannot or will not avail themselves of the protection of U.S. laws. Not only do they suffer, but so too does U.S. society."

The commission pointed out that illegality breeds illegality. In other words, the presence of great numbers of undocumented aliens has resulted in disregard not only for immigration statutes and laws against smuggling, but also in the breaking of minimum-wage and occupational-safety laws.

After reviewing what it termed the "intolerable conditions" brought about by illegal immigration, the commission made several recommendations. In order to bring illegal immigration under control, the Border Patrol should be expanded and provided with all the helicopters, patrol cars, listening devices, and other equipment needed to effectively foil border crossings and to apprehend undocumented aliens who do manage to enter the United States. As a further curb, the commission recommended the establishment of interior controls under the jurisdiction of the Immigration and Naturalization Service. An automated system for checking documents would enable the immigration authorities to trace and apprehend aliens who remain in the United States after their visas expire.

The most drastic suggestion for putting an end to illegal immigration was aimed at Americans who employ undocumented aliens. The commission maintained that since illegal immigrants come to the United States in search of work, the best way to keep them out of the country would be to deny them employment. The commission recommended legislation that would make employers subject to fines and possibly to imprisonment if they made a practice of hiring illegal immigrants.

But employers could not be punished for hiring undocumented aliens unless they were provided with the means to screen out such persons, so the commission recommended "some system of secure identification." The commission did not specify whether it thought that system should be a "counterfeit-resistant" identification card, or a computer that employers could call in the same way that business concerns now call a computer to verify a person's credit-card data.

The Hesburgh commission proposed that once illegal immigration was curbed, amnesty be granted to most of the undocumented aliens already in the country. "Qualified aliens would be able to contribute more to U.S. society once they came into the open." Having been granted legal status, such "aliens would no longer contribute to the depression of U.S. labor standards and wages."

*   *   *

Shortly after the Hesburgh commission recommended comprehensive immigration legislation to Congress, President Reagan made proposals of his own. While campaigning as the Republican nominee in 1980, he had promised to bring about an improvement in Mexican-American relations if he was elected. More specifically, he had called for an immigration policy that would permit thousands of Mexicans to enter the United States legally to work on a temporary basis. In a television interview, the future president said that he was "very intrigued" by a proposal to legalize what was then unlawful migration by granting visas to Mexicans who wanted to go back and forth across the border while holding jobs in the United States.

One of President Reagan's first acts after his inauguration was to appoint a cabinet-level committee to make proposals for new immigration legislation. The recommendations of this committee formed the basis for the Reagan administration's immigration policy, which the president announced on July 30, 1981. Several proposals that the chief executive urged Congress to enact into law were similar to those made by the Hesburgh commission. (For example, the Reagan administration suggested that Congress "recognize reality" by granting legal status to undocumented aliens living in the United States.) But two highly restrictive conditions were to apply to most illegal aliens, including undocumented Mexicans. Such persons would have to reside in the United States for ten years before they would become eligible for permanent resident status, and during that period they would not be allowed to bring their spouses or children to this country.

President Reagan also asked Congress to enact a law that would prohibit employers from knowingly hiring illegal aliens. The responsibility for determining the job applicant's status would be left to the employer. Yet the president rejected the idea of an identification card to be carried as proof of citizenship.

Two features of the Reagan policy differentiated it from the proposals made by the Hesburgh commission The president asked Congress to raise the quota for legal immigration from Mexico from 20,000 yearly to double that number. He also proposed a two-year experimental program for admitting 50,000 "guest workers" annually. In a sense, the president recommended a revival of the *bracero* program described in chapter 3.

Reaction to the Reagan proposals was mixed. Several historians who had studied the original *bracero* program observed that alien worker programs are easier to start than to control. They pointed out that "guest worker" programs ordinarily stimulate unlawful migration. They predicted that thousands of workers would be attracted to the border, hoping to take part in the proposed program. Most of those who failed to be accepted as "guest workers" would enter the United States on their own.

According to other critics of the Reagan proposals, illegal immigrants can be discouraged from entering the United States *only* if jobs are denied them. They say that employers must be required to hire only applicants who can produce counterfeit-proof identification, such as the plastic photo I.D. cards that the U.S. Department of Agriculture requires the recipients of food stamps to present. In other words, Congress has no right to penalize employers for hiring illegal aliens, unless it requires prospective workers to present foolproof identification.

Conflicting views on the "guest worker" proposal were put forward by various senators. Senator Edward Kennedy questioned Reagan's justification for admitting tens of thousands of Mexican workers when many times that number of Americans were unemployed. But Senator Harrison

Schmitt of New Mexico asserted that there were at least a million jobs that Americans could not or would not fill.

Immigration officials welcomed the president's proposal to strengthen the Border Patrol with more agents, and to build new detention centers for illegal aliens. But organizations representing the interests of illegal aliens were sharply critical of Reagan's proposals. The president of the League of United Latin American Citizens (LULAC), the largest Hispanic organization in the United States, declared that requiring illegal immigrants to live in this country for ten years before becoming permanent legal residents would be unfair. The several million aliens waiting for legalization would pay Social Security, income, and other taxes but would be denied welfare, federally assisted housing, food stamps, and unemployment insurance.

Officially, the Mexican government made no comment on President Reagan's new immigration policy. Unofficially, government leaders, conservative newspaper editors, and other members of the "establishment" expressed relief that more drastic curbs on illegal migration had not been proposed. They regarded closing the "safety valve" as a threat to Mexican stability. But writers in Mexican anti-establishment newspapers and magazines concurred with their American counterparts in contending that, in the long run, large-scale illegal migration harmed Mexico more than it harmed the United States. As long as hundreds of thousands of its citizens were able to seek economic refuge across the border, the Mexican government could avoid confronting two basic domestic problems: bringing the explosive population increase under control, and exploiting the vast wealth of Mexico for the benefit of the many instead of for the few.

* * *

Like the recommendations of the Hesburgh commission, the proposals of the Reagan administration have caused thoughtful Americans to consider the implications of the continued entry of millions of legal and illegal aliens—not just from Mexico, but from other parts of the world as well.

The traditional belief that the United States, land of opportunity and haven of the oppressed, should continue its generous immigration policy is increasingly challenged. In the past, proposals to curb immigration were made principally by racists, religious bigots, or super-patriots. But in the last few years, numbers of government officials and civic leaders have expressed the view that the United States is no longer able to assimilate the immigrants who are entering the country in unprecedented numbers. Richard D. Lamm, the governor of Colorado, recently pointed out that "it is usually not recognized, but the nation's largest number of immigrants came not in 1893 or 1911 but in 1980." According to Lamm, 808,000 legal immigrants entered the United States in 1980—this was twice the number accepted by all the other nations of the world combined. And, as the governor noted, the number of immigrants who entered illegally probably exceeded the number who entered lawfully. "Few issues facing the United States are as important as the question of immigration, and in no other are we so blinded by our past myths." After saying that "it is immensely difficult to come to grips with the new realities that face us," Governor Lamm called upon Congress to place rational limits on immigration—which means not overwhelming the Land of Liberty with more immigrants than it can absorb.

The sharpening debate on American immigration policy is leading to a reexamination, on both sides of the border, of relations between Mexico and the United States. Much attention was paid Reagan's "guest worker" proposals when the border governors of Mexico and the United States met in El Paso in October, 1981. At that conference, the governors of Mexican states along the border focused attention on the ill-treatment that many illegal aliens receive in the United States. The American governors stressed the socio-economic problems created by undocumented Mexicans living in their states.

In recent years, the issues raised by large-scale illegal immigration have received more publicity in the United States than other Mexican-American problems have received. But American leaders have been equally concerned with less publicized conflicts between their country and Mexico—for example, the unwillingness of the Mexican government to increase oil production and to sell a higher percentage of its exported petroleum to the United States. The Mexican stand on this matter has thwarted American efforts to become less dependent upon the Middle East as a source of energy.

Some American statesmen regard the conduct of Mexican foreign policy as detrimental to the United States. For instance, when Fidel Castro established a dictatorship in Cuba, the United States attempted to overturn the Communist-

FACING THE REALITY
OF MEXICO

Illegal immigration: House votes funds for more
the Mexican perspective personnel to police border

Illegal Migrants: Victims and Scapegoats

"People Feel the Entire Immigration System Is Out of Control"

Illegal Aliens Are Bypassing Farms For Higher Pay of Jobs in the Cities

No End of Woes in Coping With Aliens

Illegal aliens come cheap

Punish Employers of Illegal Aliens? To Turn the Illegal Tide

Reagan Advised to Admit Mexicans as Guest Workers

Adviser to Mexican Government Assails Reagan Immigration Plan

U.S. Hispanic Populace Growing Faster Than Any Other Minority

Hispanic Voters in California Gaining Strength in State and Local Politics

San Antonio's Battle to Blend Rival Cultures

A Spanish Course For Texas Schools

If education in Spanish is a right, the melting-pot principle is in serious danger.

Mexico, Braced by Oil, Steps Out in Foreign Affairs

Mexico: Another Worry For President-Elect

MEXICO
A New Leadership Role

Mexico: Can We Become Partners?

INTEREST AND CONCERN. These headlines from recent newspapers and magazines call attention to the gravity of Mexican-American problems and the interest in solving them. *Collage by the author*

dominated regime. As part of that effort, the United States persuaded most of the other Latin American countries to break their political and economic ties with Cuba. In this way, the United States hoped to isolate what was regarded as a satellite of the Soviet Union. But Mexico refused to follow the lead of the United States, and remained on friendly terms with the Castro government. In 1981, President Reagan accused Fidel Castro of supplying arms to the leftist guerrillas of El Salvador. The chief executive sent a delegation to the Mexican capital to try to persuade President López Portillo to support American claims against the Cuban government. In what was regarded as a rebuff to the Reagan administration, President López Portillo went out of his way to stress the close ties between his country and Cuba. At the same time, he cautioned the United States against military intervention in El Salvador.

Interestingly, criticism of Mexican foreign policy seldom appears in American publications that deal with international affairs. The stability of the Mexican government itself is even less frequently questioned—on the contrary, Mexico is generally described as the most stable nation in Latin America. In 1981, when President López Portillo named his successor and the Institutional Revolutionary Party (PRI) automatically ratified his choice as its candidate, American newspapers called attention to the fact that Mexican presidents come to power by election, rather than by military coup, as in most Latin American countries. Some commentators went on to say that PRI had won every presidential election since 1929. *The New York Times* ran this headline: "Mexico's 1982 Election: All Over but the Shouting," and its correspondent, Alan Riding, described the PRI candidate, Miguel de la Madrid Hurtado, as "the man certain to rule Mexico between 1982 and 1988." The statement emphasized the fact that while Mexican presidents are officially elected, they actually are imposed on the country by the ruling party, and de la Madrid did, indeed, win his country's presidential election in 1982.

TIJUANA MEETING. President Reagan, left, and Mexican President-elect de la Madrid walk toward the Benito Juarez Statue in Tijuana, in October 1982. The two leaders then left Tijuana for Coronado, California, and there continued talks.

Wide World Photos

For more than 50 years, Mexico has been spared the political upheavals that have all but destroyed a number of other Latin American nations. As a consequence, the United States has enjoyed the security afforded by the stability of a nation with which it shares a 2,000-mile unfortified boundary. But the stability provided by half a century of rule by one party is now threatened by a number of developments, according to some experts on Mexican affairs. Paying for its imports of food and manufactured products and servicing its soaring foreign debts requires more money than Mexico earns from its exports, including petroleum and natural gas. As a result, the Mexican balance-of-payments deficit is dangerously high, in the opinion of some economists. Mexico is also troubled by a very high inflation rate that undermines the economy. And massive unemployment, the widening gulf between rich and poor, inadequate public services, and widespread corruption have produced mounting discontent among a large segment of the Mexican population. Such conditions threaten the stability of Mexico, which Americans have long taken for granted.

The most pointed criticisms of the Mexican government are made by its own citizens. A number of Mexican intellectuals maintain that the promises made during the protracted revolution remain unfulfilled, and that until the provisions of the constitution of 1917 are carried out, their country will become increasingly unstable. These same Mexican critics are likely to add, however, that their government has little control over some of the forces that affect the socioeconomic system. Decisions made in New York and Washington often determine Mexican policy. The granting or denial of a multi-million-dollar loan by an American bank, the release or withholding of American technology, and the increase or decrease of quotas or duties on Mexican products admitted to the United States are examples of American decisions that influence, and sometimes determine, decisions made by the Mexican government.

It is not just the overwhelming economic power of the United States that Mexican officials must take into account when they determine policy. The overshadowing military might of the United States also affects Mexican decisions, particularly those relating to Central America and the Caribbean region.

Many Mexicans have long resented what they consider the subordinate role their country plays in its relationship with the United States. That resentment increased when a financial crisis developed in Mexico in the summer of 1982, and President López Portillo had to ask the United States for what some newspaper editors described as a "bail out."

Several leading economists attributed the threatened catastrophe to developments that occurred after Mexico began to exploit its vast petroleum resources. The newfound wealth brought about the rapid development of Mexican industry with the aid of equipment and technology imported from abroad.

Mexican credit was good because of the nation's exports of oil and natural gas. Foreign banks, most of them American, made multi-million-dollar loans to the Mexican government for public works and to Mexican industrialists to expand production. By 1982 Mexico had the largest foreign debt ($81 billion) of any developing nation in the world.

As long as the price of oil was high, certain danger signals could be ignored. But since 75 percent of Mexican export earnings were derived from petroleum, the sharp drop of oil prices in 1980–81 had a disastrous effect. For one thing, paying interest on loans and retiring the principal became increasingly difficult. Meanwhile, the inflation rate climbed above 100 percent, and the value of the Mexican peso declined drastically in relation to the American dollar. Many affluent Mexicans, losing faith in the national economy, tried to protect their wealth by sending it abroad. In 1982, President López Portillo estimated that Mexican citizens had invested $25 billion in American real estate, and that their other holdings abroad, principally in the United States, amounted to approximately $14 billion.

It was this flight of Mexican capital abroad that caused President López Portillo to take drastic measures to save the national economy from collapse. He appeared before the Mexican congress and with the tacit approval of his hand-picked successor, Miguel de la Madrid Hurtado (1982–1988), announced that all the private banks owned by Mexican citizens were to be taken over by the government, as the oil industry had been nationalized in 1938. He accused the private banks of encouraging Mexican citizens to send their money abroad, thus undermining the national economy.

In a plea for American cooperation, López Portillo asked for a meeting of members of the U.S. Congress with members of the Mexican legislature to discuss the flight of wealth across the border, which he said "is a more serious problem for us than the traffic of drugs is for them." But the Mexican president called for more than legislative cooperation. He sent his finance minister to Washington to ask for economic assistance. It was quickly forthcoming in the form of a billion-dollar advance payment for Mexican oil, and a billion-dollar credit to cover grain imports from the United States.

But there was more to the Mexican president's speech than a request for loans and postponement of the repayment of debts. He stressed Mexican independence by criticizing the policy of the United States in Central America, and by promising that the national government would never attempt to prevent its citizens from leaving their country for the United States. "There will be no walls. We will never patrol our own borders."

But the Mexican president had reassuring words for Americans. He underscored the fact that the United States remained a cornerstone of Mexican foreign policy. While admitting that serious economic problems persist, the president said that political relations between the two countries had been transformed. "Mexico now diverges, converges, and, above all, negotiates with the United States with dignity, respect, and friendship."

For Additional Reading

Acuña, Rodolfo. *Occupied America: The Chicano's Struggle Toward Liberation.* San Francisco: The Canfield Press, 1972.

Baird, Peter, and McCaughan, Ed. *Beyond the Border: Mexico and the U.S. Today.* New York: North American Congress on Latin America, 1979.

Bazant, Jan. *A Concise History of Mexico from Hidalgo to Cárdenas, 1805–1940.* London: Cambridge University Press, 1977.

Briggs, Vernon M.; Fogel, Walter; and Schmidt, Fred M. *The Chicano Worker.* Austin: University of Texas Press, 1977.

Cornelius, Wayne A. *Building the Cactus Curtain: Mexican Migration and U.S. Responses from Wilson to Carter.* Berkeley: University of California Press, 1980.

Davidson, John. *The Long Road North.* Garden City, N.Y.: Doubleday & Company, 1979.

Ehrlich, Paul R.; Bilderback, Loy; and Ehrlich, Anne H. *The Golden Door.* New York: Ballantine Books, 1979.

Galarza, Ernesto. *Merchants of Labor: The Mexican Bracero Story.*

Santa Barbara, Calif.: McNally & Loftin, Publishers, 1964.

Gruening, Ernest. *Mexico and Its Heritage*. New York: The Century Company, 1928.

Halsell, Grace. *The Illegals*. New York: Stein & Day Publishers, 1978.

Haslip, Joan. *The Crown of Mexico*. New York: Holt, Rinehart & Winston, 1971.

Johnson, William W. *Heroic Mexico*. Garden City, N.Y.: Doubleday & Company, 1968.

Kiser, George C., and Kiser, Martha W. *Mexican Workers in the United States: Historical and Political Perspectives*. Albuquerque: University of New Mexico Press, 1979.

Lewis, Oscar. *The Children of Sanchez*. New York: Random House, 1961.

McWilliams, Carey. *North from Mexico: The Spanish-Speaking People of the United States*. New York: Greenwood Press Publishers, 1968.

Meier, Matt S., and Rivera, Feliciano. *The Chicanos: A History of Mexican Americans*. New York: Hill & Wang, 1972.

Miller, Tom. *On the Border*. New York: Harper & Row, Publishers, 1981.

Moore, Joan W., and Pachon, Harry. *The Mexican Americans*. Englewood Cliffs, N.J.: Prentice-Hall, 1976.

Purcell, Susan Kaufman, ed. *Mexico–United States Relations*. New York: The Academy of Political Science, 1981.

Ross, Stanley R., ed. *Views Across the Border*. Albuquerque: University of New Mexico Press, 1978.

Ruíz, Ramón Eduardo. *The Great Rebellion: Mexico, 1905–1924*. New York: W. W. Norton & Co., 1980.

Samora, Julian, and Simon, Patricia Vandel. *A History of the Mexican-American People*. Notre Dame, Ind.: University of Notre Dame Press, 1977.

Weber, David J., ed. *Foreigners in Their Native Land*. Albuquerque: University of New Mexico Press, 1973.

Index

211

Texas Revolution, 3, 103–8
Thoreau, Henry David, 115
tourism, 161, 178
trade with U.S., 175–80, 183–84, 186
Travis, William B., 104
"tuna war," 181–83
Tyler, John, 111

United Farm Workers, 81, *88*
Vaky, Viron P., 3–4
Veracruz, *117*, 118, 151–52, *153*
Victoria, battle of, 107

Villa, Francisco "Pancho," 148–49, *149*, 153–54, 157

Weber, David J., 2–3
wetbacks, 15, 59
Whitmore, Jane, 3
Wilson, Henry Lane, 146–47
Wilson, Woodrow, 53, 150–55
World War I, 53, 154
World War II, 56

Zapata, Emiliano, 145–46, 148, 157
Zimmermann Note, 154–55

About the Author

E. B. Fincher was born in New Mexico and grew up in Texas. He was educated at Texas Technological College (B.A.), Columbia University (M.A.), and New York University (Ph.D.).

While teaching political science at the New Jersey State College at Montclair, he began a writing career. *Spanish Americans as a Political Factor in New Mexico*; *The Presidency: An American Invention*; and *The Vietnam War* are among his books.